The American Game

The American Game:

Capitalism, Decolonization, Global Domination, and Baseball

John D. Kelly

PRICKLY PARADIGM PRESS
CHICAGO

Prickly Paradigm Press, LLC
5629 South University Avenue
Chicago, IL 60637

www.prickly-paradigm.com

ISBN: 0-9761475-5-6
LCCN: 2006903876

Printed in the United States of America on acid-free
paper.

The dominant traits of our civilization need special scrutiny.

—Ruth Benedict

The Baseball World And Its Classics: Preface #1

Good pitching beats good hitting. This year's inaugural Baseball World Classic proved it, as well as instances can prove anything. Peter Gammons, the ESPN TV network's in-house baseball intellectual, got it right when he predicted that the Japanese would win because of their pitching, especially the formidable Daisuke Matsuzaka. Perhaps it would have been different if the Cubans had saved their best pitchers for the final. But they probably wouldn't have reached the final if they hadn't used their devastating pitching tandem, Yadel Marti with his stuff and

Pedro Lazo with his power, to defeat the Dominican Republic.

The Dominican batting lineup was regarded with awe. During their first game, while they dismembered a strong Venezuelan team led by Cy Young Award pitching, ESPN broadcasters debated whether their starting four hitters were the strongest in the history of baseball. Broadcaster Harold Reynolds tried to hold out for other teams, for example the Yankees. He was browbeaten by his colleagues, who argued (inaccurately) that Soriano, Tejada, Pujols, and Ortiz all averaged forty home runs a year in recent years. Reynolds relented and declared the Dominican strength unprecedented. (Without Vlad Guerrero, Manny Ramirez and other no-shows, the Dominican lineup's superiority centered on the first four; Soriano was sufficiently ineffective that Placido Polanco replaced him after a few games.) An outstanding lineup was blown away by Marti and Lazo, much as they dominated Venezuela, also, in a key game in round two.

So, the first Baseball World Classic illustrated an old adage. Good pitching does beat good hitting. What else did it prove? The Japanese won a hard-fought tournament of impressive, highly skilled baseball. Are they the best team in the world? Are they world champions? Or, to get the emphasis right, are they *really* world champions?

What really happened to baseball this year? Clearly, international, global baseball was reorganized by this curious professional tournament, conducted in Tokyo, Orlando, Arizona, San Juan, Anaheim, and San

Diego in March 2006. But into what form, and how far does it reach? How do we now rank baseball teams, nations, and leagues? What is baseball's measure of rank, its rules for play, its system for determining, in fact creating, champions and championships?

The owners and management of Organized Baseball have had a problem brewing for years: excellent baseball emerging beyond their grasp. World amateur baseball tournaments have been dominated for decades by Cuba, whose national team went undefeated across 152 games from 1987 to 1997, winning Olympic gold twice. This stunning record in a sport with uncontrollable elements is mitigated by lack of real competition. Cold War rivalries led Organized Baseball to ostracize the Cubans, and they were not engaged by professional teams, even Caribbean Winter League teams. Cuban strength is long-standing. They won seven of twelve Caribbean Series, from 1949 to 1960, invited to none since. The fiction that Cubans could not compete with professionals was exploded when two defecting stars, brothers Livan and Orlando Hernandez, were the best starting pitchers in successive World Series, leading the Marlins and the Yankees to victory in 1997 and 1998.

Meanwhile, the rosters of Organized Baseball were increasingly filled by players from the Dominican Republic, Venezuela, Japan, and other countries. As with football (soccer) and Europe, money led the world's best players to the metropolitan leagues. The story of Japanese baseball players is different, and important. After pioneer successes of Hideo Nomo and Ichiro Suzuki, Japanese baseball's

Jordan-level superstar, Yomiuri (Tokyo) Giant center fielder Hideki Matsui, became a successful New York Yankee. The drip of Japanese elite players joining the North American Major Leagues became a small stream. But Japanese players often take salary cuts in order to join the Major Leagues. This is an important victory in competitive organization for Organized Baseball, well served by a global order that gives elite players little option but to come to them, as individuals, seeking the chance to play in the world's elite leagues. What to do, then, as it becomes increasingly apparent that the weight of the world's baseball talent is raised outside North America? They staged a World Baseball Classic.

Lots of baseball circles, and different baseball circles, talk different ways about this tournament and its outcome. Here we consider baseball in social theory and vice versa. What was perhaps the first real world championship tournament had finalists, Japan and Cuba, with only two and zero Major League baseball players on their rosters. Does this mean that we, the global we, are on a new threshold of globalization of the American game, a moment in which US hegemony over the game is broken, the end of some kind of US empire? Is this a moment at which some kind of Baseball, capital-B, finally decolonizes?

Well, I hope to convince you of something very different about baseball, US hegemony, and decolonization. Also about capitalism and globalization; see the next preface. I will argue that the World Baseball Classic is the vehicle by which US "Organized Baseball" intends to take over international baseball.

This particular dimension of US global domination is now real but not yet sustained. The World Baseball Classic may routinize into another vehicle of actual US hegemony. Pursuing the history of the future we can only speculate about real consequences of Cuba's, Korea's, and Japan's success. But the momentum is tangible for this tournament, wholly owned by World Baseball Classic, Inc., which is in turn wholly owned by US-based Major League Baseball in partnership with its Players Association. I will argue that this is an extreme, indeed classic example of how economic globalization really works. Global commercial superhighways are neither natural, nor inevitable. They are built environments for commercial transaction, investment and further development, superhighways paved and even designed, by and for particular corporate consortia. And in this form they are not empires, and not reliant upon empires. They rely instead on their own precise independence, and on the capacity of the formal symmetries and independence of nation-states to mask sustained real inequality.

A picture and frame thing is going on here. It matters how the frame makes the picture, not just vice versa. The victory of Japan is highly significant. Japan's victory was followed (even preceded) by speculation about consequences of Japanese victory. What about the next tournament? As the "reigning" champions, what will Japan want? What will the vast, complex and powerful congeries of interests involved in Japanese baseball demand as victors, for the staging of the next tournament? Will the finals be held in Japan next time? Especially in light of the egregious errors of one US umpire, will the umpiring be different? Much will change. But what kind of reign is it that Japan has won?

To turn from the event to the staging, from the picture to the frame, the tournament does not now belong to the Japanese. A brand has been established,

Figure 1. WBC poster at a San Juan bus stop: flags are superimposed on the faces of Carlos Delgado, Albert Pujols, Andruw Jones and Ivan Rodriguez

the "World Baseball Classic" or WBC, with logo omnipresent at WBC sites, holding its own with flags adorning very popular merchandise. Nippon Professional Baseball can lever negotiations over the next tournament by threatening not to participate, as can to lesser degrees the Cubans, Koreans, and others. But the big picture, the real framing, the underlying structure is very different. MLB and its Players Association now own the real thing, and are self-positioned to be its ultimate beneficiaries. Without the Cubans, without the Koreans or Japanese, a "World Baseball Classic" would be cheapened, flawed, hollowed out, like the Moscow Olympics without the Americans and the Los Angeles Olympics without the Soviets. But that is a matter of degree, not kind. The World Baseball Classic is a corporate entity designed for sustainable profit-making, owned (directly, not merely indirectly like the Olympics) by other corporate entities. Without MLB and the Players Association, there will be no more WBCs. And they would be unlikely to join any other world championship format, especially now.

There is a general point here. The underlying structure, the infrastructure of competition (and commoditization) renders its significances and directs its possibilities. (There is also a second, contrapuntal and consoling point, about the pressures on and limits intrinsic to such structures. They need the things-for-themselves that they produce. Staging of Hamlet requires the prince, as they say, and in this case the needed prince is produced by a game and not a script. This modern prince is real games.) To the general point: Games require built environments. This hidden aspect, this condition of their possibility, is invariably, necessarily left out in most game theory, even when that theory guides the very architects of

Figure 2. WBC logos in English and Spanish in San Diego hotel lobby, also adorned with flags

such environments, the stagers of games. To understand actual games we need more than an economic game theory: we will also need a specifically historical realism.

Another complex example will illustrate. Soon enough I will be replacing this picture and frame thing with a more precise language grounded in social theory. But for now picture and frame, event and staging will enable us to discuss the significance of actual games by talking about some actual games. This is a royal road to my argument. Let us consider three baseball stories, all of them about Babe Ruth and Lou Gehrig striking out. I present the facts without the pitchers' names to help us consider salient differences later.

1. Tuesday, July 10th, 1934, a thirty-one year old lefthander famous for his deadly screwball took the mound against an all-star team. He gave up a single to the lead-off hitter, future Hall-of-Famer Charlie Gehringer. He walked one Heinie Manush. He then struck out Babe Ruth (on a called strike three) Lou Gehrig (swinging) and Jimmie Foxx (on three pitches). All were future Hall-of-Famers, as were Al Simmons and Joe Cronin, the first two batters in the second inning, who also stuck out. The screwballer then gave up a single to Hall-of-Famer Bill Dickey and struck out the ninth hitter, opposing pitcher Lefty Gomez. He left the game after three scoreless innings, with six strike-outs, allowing no runs. But his team lost 9-7.

2. Tuesday, November 20th, 1934, a seventeen-year-old right-handed pitcher, fresh out of high-school tournament competition, took the mound

against a traveling Major League all-star team, and in the first two innings struck out Charlie Gehringer, Babe Ruth, Lou Gehrig and Jimmie Foxx in succession. Giving up only five hits and striking out nine over nine innings, allowing no hits through the first four innings, he lost the game 1-0 on a solo home run in the seventh inning by Ruth. (Many accounts of this game both published and on the web appear to be wrong in salient details. For example most attribute the home run to Gehrig. I have prepared this summary from a contemporary news account, *The New York Times* of November 21, 1934.)

3. Thursday, April 2nd, 1931, a seventeen-year-old left-hander with a sharp-dropping slider took the mound against the New York Yankees, replacing a starter who had faced only two batters (Earle Combs had doubled, and Lyn Lary singled him in). Thus with a runner on first and none out, this rookie pitcher, who had signed a professional contract only five days before, faced Babe Ruth and then Lou Gehrig. Both struck out. According to the local newspaper, Ruth "kicked the dirt, called the umpire a few dirty names, gave his bat a wild heave, and stomped to the Yankees dugout." Gehrig had less to complain about; he swung and missed three times. After a four-minute standing ovation, the pitcher walked Tony Lazzeri, and then was removed from the game, replaced by the original starter. The Yankees eventually won 14-4.

Okay, so what? The similarities draw my attention here, ironically including the fact that none of these pitching heroics led a team to victory. A good case can be made, though, that all these performances were critical events, with significant consequences well beyond who won and lost the games at issue.

Not to rehearse things anthropologists have to say about texts, co-texts, and contexts (I promise) it matters a lot what was going on around them, to understand why these pitching performances are remembered so differently, or in case number three, not really remembered at all except in special circles very recently. The three pitchers were: *1.* Carl Hubbell, at New York's Polo Grounds in the second-ever mid-season Major League Baseball "All-Star Game," *2.* Eiji Sawamura, in a game in Shizuoka Japan, near Mt. Fuji, between a Japanese all-star team and "barnstorming" US all-stars, and *3.* Jackie Mitchell, in a late "spring training" game between the Yankees and the Chattanooga Lookouts of the Southern Association, as the Yankees traveled north toward the "opening day" of their regular season. If you were expecting that one of these would be Satchel Paige or some other Negro League pitcher, nope — surely there were similar feats in black-white barn-storming games, but I did not seek one. The irony of the obscurity of such games compared to the signifi-cance of Hubbell's would be low-hanging fruit. These three games all had specific, important historic effects.

So, let us now praise famous men, at least, two famous men, and one obscure minor leaguer. Hubbell's strike-out of the American League murderer's row is the kind of critical event that becomes famous as quintessential, an emergent para-digm, a touchstone for the measure of other performances. Good pitching beats good hitting, great pitching beats great hitting. Hubbell's domination of these All-Stars defines his career. Look at his Hall-of-Fame plaque:

> Carl Hubbell, New York N.L. 1928-1943, Hailed for impressive performance in 1934 All-Star Game when he struck out Ruth, Gehrig, Foxx, Simmons, and Cronin in Succession. Nicknamed Giants' Meal-Ticket. Won 253 games in Majors...

The hits need not come up, nor that Hubbell was pitching in his home park. (Nor the walk to Manush who, I am shocked to discover, is also a Hall-of-Famer. After all he got the walk.) It doesn't arise that these guys struck out a lot, Ruth and Foxx around 16% of regular season at-bats, Gehrig around 10%, the others 8 or 9 %, except Gehringer 4.2%. When accounts describe Hubbell's six strike-outs as an all-star record, they don't mention that it was the second-ever all-star game. The fame of the performance is over-determined by its utility.

Dramatic because it was in the "mid-summer classic"? Maybe. The opposite claim makes more sense. The Major Leagues needed dramatics to establish their mid-summer all-star game as some kind of classic ("classic," has that word already come up?) and this performance filled the bill. It seems pretty dialectical; the all-star classic heightens the drama, and the excellent performance makes the all-star game classic. Neither text nor context, neither performance nor staging, can be established or evaluated without the other (as usual). They are interdependent. (But equally so?)

So, what about Eiji Sawamura? Not the same kind of fame, exactly. Sawamura is the Cy Young of Japan, if you need ethnocentric bench-marking. What justifies this parallel is only that Nippon Professional Baseball named its annual award for best pitcher, 'their Cy Young Award,' the Sawamura Award. But Sawamura didn't win anything close to Young's 511 regular season major league games. Sawamura died young, at age 27 after only two full years pitching for the Tokyo Giants, and then parts of three others in between stints of military service. He was in a troop ship sunk by US warships near the Ryukyu Islands in December 1944. A different kind of context comes in here.

Japan is a different place than the US. The Japanese have their own Baseball Hall of Fame, launched in 1959 with self-comparison to the one in Cooperstown. (Like most people talking in the US about baseball, I frequently skip the word "national" when citing the title of the National Baseball Hall of Fame and Museum in Cooperstown. There are also baseball halls of fame in a lot of other places, including Cuba [founded 1939], Mexico, Venezuela, Canada, and Indiana. A Latin American Baseball Hall of Fame opened in San Juan in 2003.) Induction into the National Baseball Hall of Fame in Cooperstown was started in 1936 with five great players: Ty Cobb, Walter Johnson, Christy Mathewson, Honus Wagner, and Babe Ruth. The Japanese Baseball Hall of Fame began with a group of nine inductees: five were executives, founders of clubs, tournaments and leagues, and only four were players. None of the four players could offer impressive career statistics. All four were noted first of all for the same thing: their play against American teams. Three were pitchers, Sawamura and two others: Michmaro Ono, "First winner against American pro team 1922" (as the official English translation of his Hall of Fame plaque begins) and Yokio Aoi, "Pitched for Ikko (First High School) into an epoch-making victory (29-4) over the predominant YCAC (a foreigner's club in Yokohama) on May 23, 1896." The other player was Jiro Juji, whose plaque text begins, "The batterymate of legendary pitcher Sawamura in the All-Japan which played against the All-Americans in 1934" (all these are official English translations, from the web site of the Japanese Baseball Hall of Fame).

Competition with the US redefined Japanese baseball in the 1930s, not a neutral time in Japanese-American relations. Up to 1934 the centerpiece of Japanese baseball was the high-school tournament that was a focus of intense national interest. (See the books of Robert Whiting for extensive descriptions.) There was no pro league. The touring teams of US major league all-stars in 1931 and 1934 were undefeated, 17-0 and 16-0 respectively. But the thrill provided by the all-star tour and especially by Sawamura's near victory inspired the Hall-of-Famer Matsutaro Shoriki, owner of the leading Yomiuri Shimbun newspaper, to sponsor a pro team that toured the United States in 1935. Led by Sawamura's pitching, the team won 93 out of 102 games playing against semipro and Pacific Coast League teams. This team, "Dai Nippon Tokyo Yakyu Kurabu," the "great Japan Tokyo baseball club," was renamed the Tokyo

Giants during the tour. Back in Japan, in 1936 it joined other corporate-sponsored teams to found the Nippon Professional Baseball League.

Figure 3. Eiji Sawamura
(photo from http://www.robsjapanesecards.com/1934allnippon.htm)

Shades of Thomas Kuhn and his theory of normal and revolutionary science: Sawamura's consecutive strike-out run in November 1934, like Hubbell's in July that year, became a paradigm. But his was not so much quintessential as revolutionary, the first real evidence that Japanese baseball players could compete, at the highest level, against anyone (the Yankees, for instance). More a turning point than a centerpoint, it was, nevertheless a centerpoint to the planning of Matsutaro Shoriki. Sawamura's success enabled the organization of the U.S. tour by a Japanese professional team, then the building of a Japanese major league by a consortium of corporations. But, the occasion of Sawamura's success was also built by Shoriki, sponsor and promoter of the 1934 Babe Ruth tour. Can a revolutionary change in the organization of a national institution, like a sport, be occasioned by a great performance? Can it be managed by corporate executives? Which, the sponsoring corporations or the successful atheletes, are more dependent upon which, especially for the biggest things?

* * *

Jackie Mitchell helped found no leagues, and has no plaques in any hall of fame (though I wonder whether that is a matter of time). True, Jackie Mitchell struck out "only" Ruth and Gehrig. But on the other hand this was the Ruth of 1931, who struck out only 9.6% of his official at-bats in the majors that year, not the Ruth of 1934, his last year with the Yankees, who struck out 17.3% of the time. In fact, following that April 2, 1931 game, Ruth went on to a regular season with the lowest strikeouts per at-bat ratio of his career. It was as if something had made him hate striking out that year. Jackie Mitchell was a girl.

Maybe you prefer "woman," but remember, Jackie Mitchell was only 17 years old when she came in and took out Ruth and then Gehrig with her slider. Her neighbor Dazzy Vance, future Hall-of-Famer, taught her the pitch when she was five or six years old (see *www.jeanpatrick.com/jackielife.com*). Gehrig was harder to strike out in 1934; we could continue with minutiae. Let's look instead at the entrepreneur behind Mitchell's big moment, what he wanted and what he got.

If you know baseball you know something is fishy about Chattanooga's pitching changes. Chattanooga manager Bert Neihoff pulled his starter (Clyde Barfoot) after only two batters, making Ruth the first batter Mitchell faced as a professional, and repositioned Barfoot rather than removing him from the game. After the Ruth and Gehrig strikeouts, Lazzeri's walk led Neihoff to remove Mitchell. Her job was done. So, what was her job?

Before the game, Chattanooga newspapers ran stories about the first woman ever to play professional baseball. (Such topics, like black players before Jackie Robinson, will never die: currently the first woman in professional baseball is Lizzie Arlington in 1898, one game for Reading versus Allentown.) After the game the press was ecstatic, or at least some of it was. Chattanooga Lookouts owner Joe Engel got the local coverage he wanted (surprise?). Even before the game,

the *Chattanooga News* of March 31, 1931 predicted
great things:

> She uses an odd, side-armed delivery, and puts both
> speed and curve on the ball. Her greatest asset,
> however, is control. She can place the ball where
> she pleases, and her knack at guessing the weakness

Figure 4. Jackie Mitchell with team owner Joe Engel. (Courtesy Chattanooga
Regional Historical Museum)

of a batter is uncanny.... She doesn't hope to enter the big show this season, but she believes that with careful training she may soon be the first woman to pitch in the big leagues." After the game, no less than the New York Times was impressed: "Perhaps Miss Jackie hasn't quite enough on the ball yet to bewilder Ruth and Gehrig in a serious game. But there are no such sluggers in the Southern Association, and she may win laurels this season which cannot be ascribed to mere gallantry. The prospect grows gloomier for misogynists." (4.4.1931)

Or maybe not. From the *New York Daily News*, the day of the game:

The Yankees will meet a club here that has a girl pitcher named Jackie Mitchell, who has a swell change of pace and swings a mean lipstick. I suppose that in the next town the Yankees enter they will find a squad that has a female impersonator in left field, a sword swallower at short, and a trained seal behind the plate. Times in the South are not only tough but silly.

A stunt, a publicity stunt, something that intrinsically demeaned the game no matter what happened. Was that what Joe Engel wanted out of having Jackie Mitchell on his team? Ruth was a skeptic too.

Of course, they will never make good. Why? Because they are too delicate. It would kill them to play ball every day. (All quotations from *www.exploratorium.edu/baseball/mitchell/_2*.)

We will never know how Mitchell would have done in regular season Major League games, not even what "laurels" she could have won in the Southern Association in 1931. Mitchell pitched semi-pro, barnstorming baseball for the House of David team from 1933 to 1937, where the men wore long beards and sometimes played riding donkeys. In 1937 she retired at age 23, and worked in her father's optometry office, pitching locally on occasion. But she was banned from the Southern Association and the rest of Organized Baseball a few days after she struck out Ruth and Gehrig, by Baseball Commissioner Kenesaw Mountain Landis. Landis voided her Chattanooga contract, claiming that baseball was "too strenuous" for women.

A problem in management is relations between levels. In baseball, conflicts emerge between field managers, general managers, owners, leagues, players associations, commissioners, courts of law, and governments. Niehoff did what Engel wanted, but the result was nothing Landis wanted. By the 1930s a Commissioner of Baseball in the US was empowered by team owners to defend "the best interests of baseball," a fascinating moral concept.

Eiji Sawamura had an effect on Landis too: despite talk of a future Japanese-US World Series that circulated among baseball executives, and even reached Franklin Roosevelt, Landis acted as forcefully toward Japanese as he did toward women. In the 1935 winter meetings, he banned all future competition with Japan for the players whose contracts he controlled (thus the 1935 Japanese tour of the US would go 93-9; the teams in the leagues ruled by Landis would not play them). Despite the profits from touring Japan, and the spectacle potential of successful women players, Landis banned the competition. He had already banned exhibition games between Major League teams and Negro League teams, and all barnstorming by all members of teams in the World Series: he didn't, ever, want to see Major League teams or championship players losing to teams of Negros or Cubans (the institution of sharing World Series gate receipts with the players began as recompense for this second ban). Landis had been appointed amidst scandal, World Series game fixing, and no commissioner ever took protecting the purity and distinctiveness of the Major League game more seriously. Baseball games couldn't reach their potential, in Landis's world, unless women were barred and Jackie Mitchell forgotten, the Japanese kept distant, Cuban teams and Negro players excluded and ignored. A particular kind of purity and distinctiveness to the major league game was renewed and consolidated, as a vision of the best interests of the game instituted.

A vision of the best interests of every game is always instituted. And within those conditions of possibility, games do happen.

American Power, Capitalism and Games: Preface #2

People say the United States has an empire. There are variations. Some say the US is imperial without an empire. Or an empire in denial. Or it has an empire but not colonies. Or it is neo-imperial. Or it is an empire of liberty, an empire by invitation, or an informal empire. Criticism of US secret, ambivalent, or informal imperialism began from the Left early in the twentieth century. In nineteenth-century debates, the question was more open. Did reaching the Pacific exhaust US "manifest destiny"? Were other annexations wise, especially "salt-water imperialism" in light of adventures in China and Mexico? Colonization of China or Mexico never happened. But the Spanish-American War and other actions annexed Hawaii and appropriated the Philippines, Puerto Rico, and other islands useful to a navy with global reach, fulfilling the strategic vision of American military theorist Alfred Thayer Mahan — build reach, not burdens. In the 20th century, allegation of US Empire referred to more than global military bases, and became a corner-stone of Left-wing criticism of US foreign policy. One high-water mark came during the Vietnam War. The Vietnam years, my adolescence, were a time of profound alienation within the US, especially among the young, one of the rare times many US citizens looked at US policies, culture and power from without as well as from within. For a while, Americans looked at the US the way anthropologists look at societies. Disquiets arose. But life went on. The disquiets were less resolved than forgotten, formative in ways hidden in plain sight.

In the wake of 9/11, the theme of US imperial-ism returned. Many connect 9/11 to Vietnam. Some (for example the Vice-President) see a chance to condemn critics past, repudiate doubts and reject a "Vietnam syndrome." Others, for example Frankfurt School torch-bearer Wolfgang Schivelbusch, see (in his impressive reflection, *The Culture of Defeat*) a return of the repressed disquiets. But US political self-conscious-ness is different post 9/11, with a striking new dimen-sion to empire talk. The Right as well as the Left now talks of US imperialism, of actually being an empire. But from the Right some relish it. Whether the tone is self-awe, or the affected sobriety of Political Science "realism," voices from the Right tend strongly to applaud US empire as good, necessary or both. But the Left need not be stunned and stuck thereby, in a double bind, doomed to point out US imperialism while the Right celebrates it. Because — this is my baseline premise — the US is not an empire. US hegemony has its own distinct ways and means. The damage done to Latin America and other parts of the Global South cannot be undone by more decolonization, more self-determination, even more freedom. Iraq's problems cannot be fixed by re-decolonization, by pushing reset on the process creating a nation-state, and not only because an actually neo-imperial military occupation impedes real nation-making and state-formation. Criticism of imperialism in Iraq, for example, can be entirely correct that occupation and domination (and taking the oil) impede development of the special, sovereign relationship mutually constitutive of nation and state in the nation-state's grammar for politics. But efforts to clarify this fact, that the US cannot institute another state's self-determination by force, occlude our critical understanding of the logic and limits of self-determination itself. We have abundant critiques of instances of American hypocrisy, but they nibble around the edges. Focusing on errors (yes, serious errors) they miss truly tragic flaws, flaws in what is constitutive in US political vision of the good. In fact we could really use better critical understanding of the ways and means of US power.

Here we seek that understanding, by way of the past and present of baseball. I will be opening basic questions about capitalism in general, American capitalism in particular, about games and society in general, about games in the US in particular, about game theory in general, and about game theory in the 20th century US, in particular. Such a ridiculously broad and unmanageable terrain will find its feet in historical reality, by way of connected examples in the history of a real game, the one first called "the American game." We will use the history of "the American game" in America and elsewhere, to talk about the history of capitalism in America, and elsewhere. This is a short book about culture and power, capitalism and its politics. And above all about baseball.

* * *

> Where capitalism is at its most unbridled, in the United States, the pursuit of wealth, stripped of its religious and ethical meaning, tends to become associated with purely mundane passions, which often actually give it the character of sport.
> —Max Weber,
> *The Protestant Ethic and the Spirit of Capitalism*

Can we learn something about capitalism, especially as developed by the US, from baseball? Can we use one set of structured games to talk about another? Can we, thereby, outflank the naturalizers of games in theory and practice? Can we get an historical realist account of games and their growing place in history, a history of power politics as well as capitalist economics? Can baseball show us how games, and the structuring of games, is the key modality of US power?

Other roads would get us there by way of more significant landmarks. We could track the institutional history of trade and production of agricultural commodities, colonial and otherwise. We could reconsider the "banana republics" of the Americas, and their unmediated realization of limited liability in the conjuncture of large, necessary foreign capital and limited, local political autonomy. We could consider the significance of their growth under the aegis of the Monroe Doctrine, preceding by a generation the Versailles articulation of self-determination and the beginnings of the nation-state proper.

We could review Veblen's approach to the history of finance, reconsider from Veblenesque vantage the history of colonial and neo-colonial capital, the Banana Republics and even the British East India Company. We could also bring Veblen's insights forward, and reassess Pax Americana post World War II. These are things worth doing. But examining the relationship of self-determination to the legal ethics of limited liability and separate but equal, and reconsidering the relation of the history of colonialism to the history of finance, by themselves and even in combination do not illuminate the remarkable turn to the logic of games that has come to characterize what Americans renamed "free enterprise," and the practices of governments guided by game theorists.

Weber saw in the US a capitalism most unbridled, stripped of religious and ethical meaning. You can feel his disdain for its association with mundane passions, its turn toward the character of sport. The US was not the only place in which commerce, investment, politics and even war adopted the character of sport — consider "The Great Game" played by British and Russian Empires in the middle of Asia in the nineteenth century. But it was the US, in particular, that has developed game theory and practice, in commerce, investment, politics and war, the US that models and makes everyone a player.

I am not talking here about inflections or idioms, about the symbol used to refer to an underlying political economy whose rules relate things regardless of their names. I am talking about a built environment of and for actual games. For example, the global spread of US naval bases — why the US took Guam, but not China — makes sense when we glimpse of the strategic theories valuing them, starting from Mahan's Grand Strategy and Large View. The escalations in Vietnam make sense only within visions of global contests with the Soviets, Rostow to Kissinger.

Another social theorist and critic who saw into this problem was American anthropologist Ruth Benedict. Benedict saw in the 1930s that socialism was doomed, not for failure in provisioning of necessary and useful things, but a failure culturally. She argued that capitalism in the US followed rules that were not intrinsically economic, toward values that were not actually material. Comparing the US and Kwakiutl, in contrast to the Zuni, she argued in *Patterns of Culture* that for the former,

> it is clear that wealth is not sought and valued for its direct satisfaction of human needs but as a series of counters in the game of rivalry. If the will to victory were eliminated from the economic life, as

it is in Zuni, distribution and consumption of
wealth would follow quite different "laws."

Poverty and frustration follow massively, in a system
not designed intrinsically to eliminate them. But
systems designed to alleviate them lack the thrill of
victory, and could not reward virtues cultivated in a
world of risks identified, challenged and overcome.
Changing economic systems would be possible, but

> those who are obsessed with it too often imagine
> that an economic reorganization will give the world
> a Utopia out of their day-dreams, forgetting that
> no social order can separate its virtues from the
> defects of its virtues. There is no royal road to
> Utopia.

Benedict was no fan of competition. Concerning
rivalry as a human value, she was no relativist:

> Rivalry is notoriously wasteful. It ranks low in the
> scale of human values. It is a tyranny from which,
> once it is encouraged in any culture, no man may
> free himself. The wish for superiority is gargan-
> tuan; it can never be satisfied. The contest goes on
> forever.

What then is to be done? Abjuring a heroic role, not
out to replace capitalism or overturn US power, we
can still try to understand it. If both economic and
cultural globalization are extensions of a US hegemony, then much is at stake in understanding the
particularities of the American game. We can still seek
to change the world, not merely to understand it, but

avoid the snare of taking up a player's role, as if we must be the heroic agent of change, rival and contender in a world of struggle. Benedict was a student of Boas, and a guiding purpose for all the Boasians, after all, is to see the structures we live by. As Boas once put it:

> In fact, my whole outlook on social life is determined by the question: how can we recognize the shackles that tradition has laid upon us? For when we recognize them, we are also able to break them.

Against Elementary Forms

Ball playing in itself probably could be traced back
to the Garden of Eden.
*—1939 Official Program of the Baseball Centennial
Celebration at Doubleday Field, Cooperstown, NY*

Throughout the world baseball today is the
personification of Americanism... American
sportsmanship, team-play, aggressiveness. The
game has earned that standing.
—Kenesaw Mountain Landis, *Play Ball — America!*

What they call "Organized Baseball" in the United
States is an association by contract of professional
leagues that share rules and procedures. These leagues
share two kinds of rules and procedures above all:

those governing play on the field, and those governing the transfer of professional players up, down and around, especially up, a ranked set of leagues dominated by the top leagues, "the Major Leagues." Organized Baseball has a long, complex history of self-organization. We will delve into that history, into the larger, world history of baseball, and into relationships between other varieties of baseball and Organized Baseball in particular.

But can we speak of what baseball itself is, before engaging complexities and distinctions between baseball inside and outside of Organized Baseball? Does baseball have an elementary form?

"Baseball" is often spoken of in the singular, usually a shorthand for Organized Baseball. For a key example, Organized Baseball has a Commissioner, still empowered to act "in the best interests of baseball." This "best interests of baseball" is a wonderful conception. The first purpose of this legalism was to free baseball's Commissioner from duty to particular interest groups, even (especially) Major League team owners. But this specification of the Commissioner's powers gave "baseball" itself tangibility and paramountcy, a strange respect. The legal document rendered it almost divine, a sports godhead. Joseph Ellis tells a similar story in *Founding Brothers* about the origin of popular sovereignty. Thomas Jefferson finessed a puzzle, whether to please Southern slave-holders by vesting sovereignty in the states, or appease Hamiltonians with a sovereign national state. In the US Constitution, "the people" were found sovereign, granting power in specified measure to states and federal government, retaining all other rights and powers. Legal charter gives baseball itself, like these people, apparently original dominion.

"Commissioner of Baseball" like many names points at a dead past. Organized Baseball has a "Commissioner" because it was once run by a commission. The 1903 National Agreement (among the teams of 15 professional leagues) created a three-person National Commission to supervise professional baseball. The scheme failed, because (reports "The Commissionership: A Historical Perspective," an unsigned article posted on MLB's website *mlb.mlb.com/NASApp/mlb/mlb/history*) vested interests of its members, officers of particular clubs, made it unworkable. After the 1919 Black Sox scandal, when White Sox players conspired with gamblers to fix and throw the World Series, a new agreement created the Commissioner of Baseball, and appointed judge Kenesaw Mountain Landis. Landis was connected to no particular club or league, and as a judge proved his sympathy for Organized Baseball by upholding Organized Baseball's anti-trust exemption in a landmark judgment in 1914. The 1921 Agreement vested him with extraordinary powers to act unfettered against anything "detrimental to the interests of baseball."

My method here is Weberian. Good questions matter. Especially when they cannot be answered adequately, they provoke inquiry. The best definitions and insights come at the end of the analysis. This method has long been scandalous when it is ever understood, and in hope of explaining and using it better this long essay begins with methodology, inter-leaved with baseball now, and capitalism next.

We can think of baseball as a genre of game. That seems safe enough. But this concept of genre is hardly innocent. We can be abstract about this: if x is a genre of y, perhaps neither x nor y can exist independently of each other, neither prior to the other. Can there be games in particular without games in general, baseball without games? One can imagine games existing without baseball certainly, but games in general without any games in particular? Do the particular games that actually exist change the content and significance of what games in general are, especially if, say, games move from one among pleasurable pastimes to become, also, core mechanisms for competitive allocation of commodities and capital? Or more prosaically, do games change after team sports emerge among genres of games? If things start general and grow in their particulars, or start in isolated particulars and aggregate into more general phenomena, then tracking a history of things, having theories of their evolution, and so on, would be a lot easier. Either way would be okay, even both on occasion, as long as it was one, or the other. But what if the processes don't divide neatly, or the beginnings aren't elementary?

Mikhail Bakhtin called genres the drive-belts of history. He objected with intellectual firepower to the argument that change in language was the result of drift. Bakhtin argued that there was no general flow of speech, no speech in general. All language in use came in genres, and the rules, fashions, practices, and struggles reshaping speech, in short the poetics and politics of speech, centered on genre histories. This concept of genre can be used effectively for more than language, genre as organized particular type, thus baseball as a genre of games much like novels are a genre of discourse. The concept of genre and much else in Bakhtin's analytics gives us a different entry point into baseball history than search for an essence in origins, eternals, or elements.

Baseball is not the drive-belt of history. There are too many books arguing that baseball is the center of American culture. I am not sure cultures have centers; this idea of baseball's cultural centrality (and US centrality to baseball) interests me more as a piece of ideology than an assessment of it. To some extent, games, the larger genre, are now a drive-belt of history. Games are now deliberately extended through our world to change it, as for example the Cold War competitions reshaped decolonization, a drive belt in our new world order. But let us stick with baseball for a while longer.

How can we tell whether something is or is not baseball? Can we simply let any old thing be base-ball that says or thinks it is? Okay, my respect for Bruno Latour and his arguments notwithstanding, let's not have the games thinking themselves, when in fact, in a Game Theory variation on Heisenberg, the observers construct the games they see. I am sympa-thetic with most of Latour's irreductive methodology. But games that naturally think themselves sounds to me like something deeply within contemporary Economics, games found naturally and inevitably everywhere, especially as they are constructed. To

rephrase, then, can we simply let anything be baseball
that somebody says is baseball? How can we tell what
is real baseball and what isn't? Can we decide that
baseball is whatever this Commissioner is willing to
recognize as baseball? You already know about the race
line and the Negro Leagues, and Jackie Mitchell's
contract being voided, and Landis banning MLB players from barnstorming in Japan. So we can get quickly
past the perils of simplicity and sin of innocence here.
It is definitely no use just trusting the Commissioner.
Happy Chandler, successor to Landis as Commissioner
and one-time US Senator from Kentucky, is widely
respected in baseball history for not invoking "the best
interests of baseball" clause to prevent Jackie Robinson
from breaking the color bar in 1947. But he did invoke
the clause starting in 1946, to ban players effectively
for life who signed contracts to join teams in the
Mexican League. In 1947 Chandler was in Cuba,
trying to persuade Cuban professional team owners not
to employ "jumpers" who had left Organized Baseball
for Mexico. Baseball was "an American sport that had
to be played by American rules," he argued (I suspect
the rule he had uppermost in mind was the reserve
clause). As González Echevarría records (in *The Pride of
Havana: A History of Cuban Baseball*) Chandler told the
Cuban club owners that "American baseball was the
only clean baseball. Such pronouncements did not
make many friends for Chandler, who left Havana
without an agreement."

 Bakhtin had good methodological advice: to
understand genres, it is better to start with complexity
than simplicity. Complex genres include others within

them. Novels can include love letters, unspoken
thoughts, and lots of dialogue, baseball includes throw-
ing and running, and more than this, fully fledged
games within and across the game, base-stealing, working the count, platooning, trading players between
teams. Complex genres, Bakhtin advised, are capable of
sustaining and objectifying human reason and will,
attracting and advancing human deliberation, planning,
intention. Language and other institutions in history
are more than a drift of forms changing arbitrarily,
because genres become engines of developmental
action. Political speeches, scientific treatises, novels, in
turn become part of larger discursive institutions:
campaigns, sciences, arts.

Complexity makes definition problematic.
Origins are not essences, yes, and given the compound
nature of complex genres unitary origins are unlikely
(the first political speech, the first work of art). But if
this seems an invitation to murk, it is the opposite.
Starting in the middle, accepting that complexity is
important and intrinsic, is the beginning of wisdom.
One can then expect particular coordinates. As Bakhtin
put it, there are centripetal and centrifugal forces.
Nothing is completely or exclusively organized, nor is
any action outside of all organization. For any complex
form of articulated human agency, there are likely to
be aspects of context that bind it, interpret it, control
it, and invest it with significance according to given,
existing orders of rules, examples, other historic
instances, and above all, in all likelihood, an institutional history. Policers of the genre. Forces out to
make sure that baseball games are just so, a baseball

game like others, in line with others. Yes, baseball has such forces of organization. For comparisons sake, there was a Catholic Church in the late medieval world of prayer, ritual and text that Bakhtin observed in his book *Rabelais and His World*. But that Church was not everything. There were other kinds of speech, even other kinds of prayer, and Rabelais in his novels incorporated variety and parodies of language forms of all authorities of his day. New Christianities would emerge, also other new forms of authority, language and truth that were vernacular and secular in Europe's emerging Renaissance.

Baseball is not remotely as complicated, filled with cross-currents and counter-authorities as late medieval European religious truth. In contemporary baseball the rivals to US-based Organized Baseball, the counter-forces for centripetal organization and reorganization of the game, are mainly East Asian baseball (from the Taiwanese little leaguers of the last four decades to this year's World Baseball Classic professionals) and Latin American and Caribbean baseball, most threatening at its Cuban extreme. In a less threatening exterior, amateur baseball feeds and complements professional baseball in many loosely related kinds from little league and legion ball to the NCAA. Amateurs also provide some minor rivalry to the pros, via open world championships, the World Cup, and baseball in the Olympics. More complicated centripetal and centrifugal forces exist in sports more broadly, entertainment more broadly than that, and capitalism more broadly still. A burgeoning literature now compares different sports and their global histories and

politics — see the books by Allen Guttmann, and
Markovits and Hellerman's *Offside: Soccer and American
Exceptionalism*, Szymanski and Zimbalist, *National
Pastime: How Americans Play Baseball and the Rest of the
World Plays Soccer*, and Franklin Foer, *How Soccer
Explains The World*. Hollywood, television, and the
broader history of entertainment and leisure have their
own histories too. The history of studio contracts for
movie stars, for example, could illuminate by comparison the history of the reserve clause and free agency.
But this study will focus on baseball and American
capitalism, via the capitalism in Organized Baseball. It
won't compare global sports and entertainment organizations, except for occasional comments especially
where they influence Organized Baseball's own global
strategy.

So, for any genre in practice, centripetal forces
are unifying projects, but they are not always unified.
An authority can be challenged by an outside authority.
One institutional complex that sets rules and meanings
and gives shape and location to an activity can be challenged by others. (Is this an official game, a league
game — for which league? Is the Olympics the world
championship? Really?) But Bakhtin saw more than
this. The centripetal forces aren't the only ones. Style,
innovation, resistance, friction, interruption, avoidance,
parody, all these things by design and by accident,
especially with all the gray areas at the joints between
the pieces making up complex genres, make every
instance unique, contextually specific, irreducibly
different. Baseball broadcasters are wont to observe, at
least since Vin Scully's day, that if you pay attention

you will see something you have never seen before in every baseball game you watch. In complexity lies potential. Thus the enormous energies devoted to organizing it, and analyzing it critically, and trying to do things with it (like get a new perspective on capitalism and American power).

So, baseball is a genre of game. There is a dauntingly large literature on its origins, and we turn briefly to the beginnings of the game, to finish this reversal of Durkheim's theory of "elementary forms": elements require larger organization, which is never absolute. Next section we reconsider the commodity and its secrets in this light, in particular the commitment of Marx and others to the commodity as the elementary form of capitalism. Baseball first.

* * *

To be efficient, here are several pieces and several puzzles too.

A sign at City Hall in Hoboken, New Jersey reads, "The Birthplace of Baseball." A plaque at Doubleday Field in Cooperstown, New York describes it as "The Birthplace of Baseball" and "A National Shrine." The mayor of Pittsfield, Massachusetts, James Roberto, has declared that "Pittsfield is Baseball's Garden of Eden" (*The Boston Globe* May 11, 2004). There is trouble with all these claims: literary sightings predate them. Jane Austen, in a 1798 draft of her novel *Northanger Abbey*:

It was not very wonderful that Catherine, who had by nature nothing heroic about her, should prefer

cricket, baseball, riding on horseback, and running
about the country at the age of fourteen, to books.

Austen fans are prone to boast that this is the first literary reference to baseball. It depends what you mean by
literature. *A Little Pretty Pocket-Book* (England, 1744)
includes a poem with a woodcut illustration of a game
that lacked bats, but involved striking a ball and
running from post to post until returning "Home with
Joy"; the poem was called "Base-Ball."

Where was the first real baseball game played?
Is it an English game, or American, or Native
American? Is it rural or urban?

Looking for the origins of baseball you wade
through mythos. Because the game unravels as you go
back, you can track a history for any of its parts. In the
routes you take, you express yourself. My wife, another
anthropologist, wonders whether league play and even
regular seasons began with the Iroquois ball games.
Native Americans definitely had games with balls and
sticks played by teams in warlike style, representing
towns and sometimes nations, with bets and prizes at
stake (See Thomas Vennum, *American Indian Lacrosse:
Little Brother of War*). In the case of the Iroquois, on
occasion teams represented nations within the confed-
eracy in brutal games called to resolve political issues,
within a league (interesting term) that had banned war.
This team sport, this so-called "lacrosse" was observed
as early as 1630, so named by French missionaries. As
the name "lacrosse" suggests, the missionaries were
reminded of something by the shape of the sticks. But
to paraphrase Montaigne: what's the use, they don't

wear breaches. In keeping with my larger theme, it is actually wisest to understand the history of the quest for the origin of baseball.

*　*　*

The story that Abner Doubleday invented baseball in Cooperstown, New York in 1839 is discredited. The original source was a letter by a guy named Abner Graves, who claimed that Abner Doubleday laid out a new kind of field for town ball, a diamond, and declared the new game "base ball" in 1839 in Cooperstown, New York. More recent observers, paying attention, have noticed a few details that cast doubt on Graves's story. Graves was actually the same age as a cousin of Civil War General Abner Doubleday, a cousin fifteen years younger, also named Abner Doubleday. A tale of three Abners. The Civil War soldier Abner Doubleday, long out of diapers in 1839, was not in Cooperstown that year.

What should have given away the Doubleday story all along was the Cooperstown connection. James Fennimore Cooper, lake district tourism. What a coincidence. Or, as Jim Gates, library director, National Baseball Hall of Fame and Museum (in Cooperstown) said to *The Sarotogian*, a local newspaper (published April 3, 2005), "As someone once told me, if baseball wasn't invented here, it should have been.... It's the perfect setting for the Hall of Fame." Cooperstown regulates folklore, telling and re-telling, with special emphasis on "the national." Gates inserted the national dimension, commenting on Pittsfield in the same interview:

"That's the latest discovery," Gates said. "We look forward to the next one. There is no specific birth-place or birth date. Baseball evolved from a variety of stick-and-ball games played at various places *throughout the nation*" (my italics).

There is a long history to shaping national patrimony by asking about the origin and essence of baseball. The Doubleday story was promoted by the Mills Commission, which worked from 1905 to 1907, sponsored by sporting-goods manufacturer Albert Spalding. The Mills Commission was created to find baseball's origins. Like current Hall Of Fame leader-ship (check the resume of President Dale Petroskey) the military men, politicians and businessmen of the Mills Commission leaned Right in politics. In fact it was built to respond to a specific threat: the allegation of Henry Chadwick, prominent early baseball promoter and a known Englishman, that baseball had its roots in the English game of rounders. Chadwick, a journalist and author, was a leading nineteenth-century baseball intellectual. He invented, or at least routinized, batting averages, ERAs (earned run aver-ages), and box scores. He was important enough in the history of the game that he is a Hall of Famer himself, inducted in 1938, his plaque declaring him "Author of the first rule-book. In 1858 chairman of rules committee in first nation-wide baseball organi-zation." Centripetal force embodied, authority enshrined. But the rounders thing had to go.

Cooperstown connects the origin of baseball to national culture, and to the idea that the nation has

— or should have, a wonderfully distinct conception
— rural roots. In *The Sarotogian*, Tim Wiles, the Hall's
director of research, explained the rural roots:

> "You have to have a starting point."

> If nothing else, Cooperstown perpetuates the
> romantic notion of small-town, rural boys playing
> baseball on idyllic summer afternoons. Movies such
> as *Field of Dreams* and *The Natural* wouldn't have
> the same impact if it could be proved that baseball
> was invented in New York City's Hell's Kitchen, for
> example.

> "Clearly, there were kids like Abner Doubleday
> playing baseball," Wiles said. "The roots of the
> game extend back to places like Ballston Spa and
> Cooperstown. This is the kind of place where base-
> ball could have originated. It's a good representa-
> tion of where baseball comes from."

The Hall debunks the Doubleday story in its own
displays, and never inducted him. It no longer displays
what it once called "the Doubleday baseball," a very
dead looking hand-stitched ball found in a farmhouse
in Fly Creek, NY, three miles from Cooperstown. Its
exhibit "From Bat and Ball to Baseball" (viewed by my
daughter Nory and me in April 2006) now demon-
strates connections after all to rounders and stool ball
and other British games, including the 1744 poem,
and then goes earlier, finding a deep (but wholly
European) cultural genealogy, tracking to ball games
in French monasteries, a Spanish church manuscript
from 1251, and Pharaoh Tutmose III in 1460 B.C.,

clearly depicted on his tomb holding a bat and ball for a ritual or game called seker-hemat.

The National Baseball Hall of Fame and Museum promotes the national story but also reaches upstream to an almost unassailable headwater. Ben Eastman tells me that the Cuban government promotes a connection to a Taino (Caribbean native) bat and ball game conveniently called "batos," as Ben puts it "a way to both strengthen Cuban claims and mitigate the anxiety of American origins at the core of Cuban cultural and political forms." Tutmose does less for any nation — perhaps, as Steve Martin said of King Tut, he now dies for tourism — but the Hall takes the national connection as seriously as ever. It now reverses the proposition, looking not for an American origin for baseball but a baseball origin for America. Its recent book and traveling show, "Baseball as America," joins the many efforts to place baseball at the center of US cultural history.

Let this bring us back to Jane Austen and Pittsfield, and before them the poem in 1744. This poem and woodcut pretty clearly described the game usually called "stool ball," named after stools because players often used stools for the posts. The poem made its game "Base-Ball" an allegory for Britons pursuing "Lucre" and returning back again, so if we want we can declare that baseball is actually, intrinsically, allegorical imperialism; but let's not. Stool ball is part of the children's-games genealogy of cricket as well as baseball, in a wide field of related games. (An 1834 advice book published in Boston, *The Book of Sports*, included rules for "base or goal ball" that were a direct reprint of rules published in London in 1828 in *The Boy's Own Book*, for "rounders.") The breadth and disorder of the set is well illustrated by the 1791 Pittsfield ordinance, clearly out to lump together and ban all ball games:

> no person an Inhabitant of said Town, shall be permitted to play at any game called wicket, cricket, base ball, bat ball, football, cat, fives, or any game with a ball within the distance of 80 yards...

...of the meeting house with new glass windows.

So, Hoboken. As Warren Goldstein details in *A History of Early Baseball*, 1840s and 1850s baseball clubs were clubs in the ordinary sense, mixing banquets with their home-and-home contests. In the annals of simplicity a leader of such a club, one Alexander Cartwright, has come to succeed Abner Doubleday as the inventor of baseball because of rules he wrote or helped write for the Knickerbocker Base Ball Club of New York, which he founded or helped found in 1845. The US Congress found time, in 1953, to name Cartwright "the Father of the modern game." It helped that his Knickerbocker club played in Hoboken at "the Elysian Fields." Some versions of the Cartwright story make the Knickerbockers the first real, organized baseball club and a Knickerbocker game in Hoboken on June 19, 1846 the first real, organized game. This story has a problem similar to the one in Genesis, about the origins of Cain and Abel's wives. In their great inaugural game, the Knickerbockers lost, to the "New York Nine," and they lost 23-1.

British or American, rural or urban? National or what? The routinization of the rules and the formation of organizations tell the real tale. Most careful baseball historians locate the origin of the game in urban spaces. David Voigt (in *American Baseball*, volume II) writes that baseball:

> grew to fit the leisureways of an increasingly urban America where an ethic of fun was gaining at the expense of such values as religious sobriety and commitment to toil. Certainly by the 1840s, and probably earlier, the basic pattern of the game was shaped in the snobbish gentlemen's clubs which vied with one another for championship honors in several eastern cities. By 1845 one of these clubs, the New York Knickerbockers, established the dimensions of the baseball diamond and thus created the familiar battlefield for all baseball games to this day. As other aspiring gentlemen formed exclusive clubs in America's northeast and old northwest, they adopted the "New York Game" of the Knickerbockers, thereby making it the basis for intercity competition. Such contests attracted throngs of urbanites, and by 1860 a national mania surrounded these clubs as they battled for the mythical championship of the United States.

A snobby gentleman's thing, gone intercity and then national by way of newspaper accounts of club rivalries. We get all the way to the "national game," a term first used in New York newspapers in 1855, "the national pastime" in 1856, without a rural root in sight (Jules Tygiel's *Pastime*).

* * *

Books are still written finding baseball's origin in rural America. There is a parable here for Elementary Forms theory, the risks in mistaking *Paradise Lost* ideology for a bridge to lost paradise, meeting American Avons while questing for Gardens of Eden. There is peril for clear understanding in seeking origins that are essences, and worse, essences that are origins. Baseball stayed amateur, clubby and gentlemanly only until it got better organized, which it did quickly. But even its high amateur days connect more closely to ideologies of rural landscape than they do to the rural landscape. The organization of baseball clubs in the nineteenth century was clearly part of the muscular Christianity movement, which spread like the game from urban, elite, and ambitious circles, planning the national destiny, to rural audiences enobled by its vision. (On "muscular Christianity," see the books of John MacAloon and J.A. Mangan.) Muscular Christianity dragged the Protestant Ethic away from dour Calvinism, away from inner-worldly asceticism and out onto playing fields. It entwined religious masculinity with patriotism, the body, and sports. Mission experience of Native American team sports may have influenced it; the main doctrines were its own new readings in Christianity. While English muscular Christians organized Europe's first team sports at Rugby and other public schools in the nineteenth century, Englishmen and others in urban America made baseball a game to test and express skill, honor, character, manliness and ambition. Muscular Christianity reworked religion, masculinity, gentlemanly status and even theodicy with games and teams in a way that reoriented all elements, emphasizing sound body for sound mind, good sportsmanship for fairness, victory as its own reward, amateurism as the moral ideal, and team spirit as the better solution for all otherworldly anxiety and quiet desperation.

Muscular Christianity may or may not be another Protestant ethic that contributed to major changes in the history of capitalism. The elective affinity of team-spirit with management is obvious and renowned. But capitalism definitely changed baseball, made it bigger, gave it new, better "best interests." Unlike sports where amateurism has had a long run (see MacAloon on the Olympic movement, and Ashis Nandy and Boria Majumdar on amateurism in cricket), in baseball, once the rules of play were fixed, the clubs themselves changed massively as amateurs met professionals in actual tests of strength. The game, the organization of the game, the professionalization of the game, and the capitalism of the game almost seamlessly connect in the emergence of baseball as we now have it; let us review what all this implies for analysis by way of elementary forms.

* * *

Emile Durkheim titled his last great book *The Elementary Forms of the Religious Life*. From the days of his doctorate, Durkheim reopened the project launched by Auguste Comte and others, a positive science of sociology that could resolve the most basic problems of humanity and philosophy. When he set out to find "the elementary forms of the religious life," Durkheim sought the simplest religion, and thought he had found it in phratry dualisms, division of all into two clans, among some Australian Aborigines. But whey did he want the simplest, and he thought, therefore closest to original, religion? He quested after "the religious nature of man" in general, something that was an "essential and permanent aspect of humanity." (I quote the Swain translation.)

Durkheim agreed with Comte about the importance of an emerging science of sociology, but disagreed about the means necessary to constitute its truths. Comte argued fiercely for study first of the most advanced society, obviously (he thought) Europe, since sociology methodologically had to put the whole before the parts and use a comparative method that was historical, locating societies in stages of general development. Only with knowledge of fully advanced society, Comte thought (in the 1840s) could one appreciate the whole historical series, with other societies placed appropriately in rank somewhere below. Durkheim thought Comte erred radically by claiming to know the whole before the parts. Aware of markedly different theories of the origin of religion, with significant flaws, Durkheim sought an empirical solution to his philosophical question. Believing that luxury comes after bare necessities (another danger-ous premise for anyone anywhere near capitalism) he sought the religion so simple that it was reduced to the essential, "the principal elements." "All is reduced to that which is indispensable, to that without which there could be no religion."

> Every time that we undertake to explain something
> human, taken at a given moment in history — be it
> a religious belief, a moral precept, a legal principle,
> an aesthetic style or an economic system — it is
> necessary to commence by going back to its most
> primitive and simple form, to try to account for the
> characteristics by which it was marked at that time,
> and then to show how it developed and became
> complicated little by little.

The force of thought is sweeping and attractive.
Durkheim was right, methodologically, that "the point
of departure" is crucial for any "series of progressive
explanations, for all the others are attached to it." He
was self-perceptive when he aligned his method with
Decartes, and then reversed Descartes on a key point,
as he did with and against Comte. There is no question, he argued, of finding the universal essentials of
religion in pure possibility, "simply by force of
thought. What we must find is a concrete reality, and
historical and ethnological observation alone can
reveal that to us."

But Durkheim was wrong to seek an elemen-
tary form of religious life, eternal and necessary to all
religions and all humanity. In quest of elementary
forms Durkheim smuggled complexity into his model
of simplicity. In his account of a simplest possible
(note the Cartesian possibility after all) yet allegedly
ethnographically existing Australian religion and society, Durkheim smuggled in a story of an annual cycle
of prescribed rituals, cosmology informing rites that
renew beliefs. Durkheim sought and found a "church"

52

as he assembled data about Australian rites, ignored actual complexities of Australian societies, and gave rites belief-regulating functions that were familiar to him from experience of Christianity. He moved the church from European history into human nature. In this critique some readers will see the influence of Talal Asad, especially his book *Genealogies of Religion*. Asad shows something particularly interesting missed by Durkheim and a century of studies of primitive religion in Durkheim's wake: "ritual," like, say, "textual" or "manual," is a derivative conception, addressing the structure of something else: rites, a text, a hand (Latin: manus). Manuals are handbooks, directing hand labor and manual labor is labor done by hand, etc. Textual things are things about or from texts. Ritual? Asad shows that "the ritual" began in the middle-period history of Roman Catholicism, as the church organized its control over religious practices. "The ritual" was a set of instruction texts that guided priests in the conduct of rites, separating the obligatory, the possible and the proscribed, describing and delimiting procedures. The idea that rites related to, controlled and renewed beliefs about cosmology (the logic of the cosmos), eschatology (logic of last things) soteriology (of salvation), deontology (of duty) — the doctors of the church really went yard on this stuff — turns out to be part of a particular institutionalization of truth and power. And having practices of priests monitored via ritual rulebooks changed what rites were: it made the ones from the ritual into the official rites of the Church, others not. Ritual texts constituted orthodoxy and distinctiveness in routines, a sort of regular season for authorized rites, league rites. All this changed the conditions of possibility for rites.

Comparing baseball and religious history gets silly very soon. Sainthood, hall of fame, canonization, induction, were the miracles authenticated? Baseball is not, actually not, a kind of religion. No, it really is a genre of game. It doesn't get more real by being shown similar in some respects to something else. My point is that religion too will not be best understood starting from rites, with an idea of primitivity laid onto Australia or Africa, the idea of church smuggled in. Religion is better studied via the ins and outs of ritual, not rites. Its point of departure should be observing, historically and ethnographically, the complex institutions that organize rites, beliefs, cosmologies, deontologies, with real institutional histories, achievements and limits in larger dialogical fields. The study of religion should begin with ritual projects, not any elementary form of rite or belief.

* * *

Henry Chadwick wrote his influential baseball rule book at an auspicious moment. In the late 1850s, 25 baseball clubs formed a National Association of Baseball Players. Most or all came from New York City, but the idea of a national game was part of their purpose in codifying rules. Chadwick by then was promoting a national game in newspapers stories, explicitly like cricket for England. The association adopted standardized rules and established the possibility of championships. But there was no "regular season" or round-robin of league play. Teams played each other on a challenge basis. The National Association began to charge admission for some games to finance its activities. Gambling on games led to profits, and even early on some star players were paid despite high hopes for amateurism and its virtues. After scandals and heated accusations of unfairness, the 1868 annual meeting undertook to restore the integrity of the amateur game, and inadvertently buried it forever: it divided the league into amateur and professional clubs. In 1869 the Cincinnati Red Stockings, led by Harry and George Wright, used gate receipts to recruit and pay the best players available and won sixty five games without a loss. The strongest clubs in the National Association declared themselves professional.

Baseball goes in many directions in the 1860s and 1870s. Universities take up the sport and found clubs, including a women's club at Vassar by 1866. Missionaries and students take the game to Japan in the 1870s and students bring the game back to Cuba at least by 1864. The Habana Base Ball Club is founded in 1868, and the game is banned by the Spanish by 1869. By 1878, Cuba has its own league with professional players and an "island of Cuba base-ball championship" tournament, only four years after a National League (that would be the National League) is founded by the Cincinnati Red Stockings and other professional clubs. Professionalism spreads unevenly: not until the 1930s in Japan, never to the schools in the US (if you believe the NCAA) but very early in Cuba and among US leagues. Where they play, the professional teams tend to win, and to push harder for more organized play. In the US, ruinous, disorganized competition for players among professional clubs and leagues lead to a series of agreements, first among professional players, then among clubs, then between leagues, leading to the National Agreements that created Organized Baseball.

Capitalism came into baseball despite the amateurism of its muscular Christianity. If you can smell moneyed interests in Cooperstown in the 1930s, they are already there with the Red Stockings in the 1860s. *Paradise Lost* stories might lead us to expect capital to ruin everything it touches. Why then does the number of leagues explode and the quality of play continually improve? Why then does professional baseball incessantly promote and distribute the agrarian roots, paradise lost stories of a more innocent yesteryear?

Much critical scholarship on capitalism and popular culture operates with its own paradise lost story. Once upon a time things were only what they were, and people liked it that way, giving each other gifts. Then capitalists showed up and commoditized things and people, taking profits and not sharing, and then... different outcomes depending on the theorist, from grim postmodernisms in which second layers of tyranny by sign systems further enslave us as consumers, to happy recoveries of agency by way of consumer self-consciousness. The commodity, like the primitive rite or that game in Hoboken, becomes the elementary form for the analysis of capitalism.

But it wasn't commoditization that changed baseball so unmistakably. It was higher levels of capi-

talist organization. Above all, the leagues changed
everything. What are they, and what is their relationship to commodities? Commoditization, yes, but we
will need more tools than that: we will need to understand whole new layers of management. We will need
a theory of the firm. Professional Sports leagues did
more than commoditize the game. They incorporated
it. What is that?

The World and Capitalism (A World Series, a Capitalist World, a Baseball World)

Stand beside her...
> —an instruction given to God in "God Bless America"

I don't care if I ever get back.
> —from "Take Me Out to the Ballgame," the most common 7th inning sing-along, sometimes played right after "God Bless America"

The first "World Series" between National League and American League champions was in 1903. Every

year since has seen one — well, except 1904 when
the NY Giants disdained it, and 1994 when labor
trouble wiped it out. Two competitions in early 2006
compare for opposite reasons. One is modeled on it,
the other not so much. In February 2006 came the
49th "Caribbean Series," an event first played 1949,
often called "The Caribbean World Series." In
March 2006 came the first "World Baseball Classic."

What is the World Series? Why is it called
that? We will begin in 2006 and end with the consolidating leagues of 1903. How did capitalist forms of
organization take over and reorganize baseball?
When, how and why did baseball become something
valuable in a capitalist world? In business-school
locution, how was value added to baseball? With
what consequences for the game? Can adding games
to the world create value? What kinds and for
whom? Value for the world? What world?

* * *

Early baseball was always already infused with
elements from capitalism. We can "follow the things"
to track what is sometimes called capitalist penetra-
tion: baseball things were for sale by the mid-19th
century, the tickets for National Association games
by 1858 at least, and players for sale by the late
1860s. Balls, bats, mitts, and uniforms are hard to
imagine as anything but commodities, thus the fasci-
nation with that lumpy, hand-stitched "Doubleday"
ball from Fly Creek, NY, its aura of pre-history.
Urban setting is another clue that baseball grows in
market soil. Even at the level of "ethics," capitalism is

always already there, or at least, baseball was always already situated allegorically toward or away from commerce, from the empire-building in *A Little Pretty Pocket-Book* to the amateur ideal of muscular Christianity.

Competent professional players began to make the game a means to profit, starting with the prowess of the Cincinnati Red Stockings. The line of movement from clubs to leagues to Organized Baseball remade baseball into an increasingly inter-connected congeries of commercial institutions, made baseball into a branch of what Americans like to call "free enterprise." Baseball reorganized from indepen-dent clubs, originally player-oriented leisure groups, into profit seeking corporations in a legally powerful cartel. We can use this history to discuss dynamics of capital, profit, and finance in the actual capitalist world. What are the key genres of capitalism, its defining institutional structures, drive belts of its history? What is baseball, when it is not only a genre of game, but also, a genre of capitalist enterprise? What then constitutes its best interests, and how?

* * *

On February 4, 2006, in game three of the Caribbean World Series, Álex González of the Venezuela Caracas Lions hit a three run home run in the top of the ninth (very close to the end of the game), turning likely defeat into victory over the favored Dominican Republic Licey Tigers. Four days later González drove in the tying run in the bottom of the ninth, then scored the winning run on the final game's final play, making the Venezuela Caracas Lions the 2006 Caribbean Series champions.

Signs are bent to the breaking point here. A "Caribbean World Series" is possible only because the other World Series has its actual scope in doubt. The Caribbean World Series borrows prestige with "World Series," yet undermines the touchstone, treating the element "World Series" as mere name, not designation of world championship. The "World" of "World Series" becomes a dead letter, the reference of "World Series" simply the championship series of US and Canadian Major League baseball. Imitation in this case is both flattery and flattening, flattening a thing into a mere name. (A series between champions of AAA leagues has been played intermittently since 1904, called the "Little World Series" until 1931, then the "Junior World Series" until 1998 when it was renamed, cleverly, the "Triple-A World Series.")

The Licey Tigers and the Caracas Lions are perfectly grammatical professional sports teams, a quasi-totemic animal more or less arbitrarily attached to the name of the city meant to rally around the ticket-selling team. But "Venezuela Caracas Lions" is strange. Their uniforms at the Caribbean Series did not say "Venezuela." Another team's road caps and uniforms did refer to their country, "Dominicano," but country-designating emblems dominated no uniforms at the Caribbean Series (unlike the World Baseball Classic, which could not do enough with flags and other national emblems). All the uniforms at the Caribbean Series carried prominent corporate advertising (versus almost no-logo uniforms worn in the

WBC). The Dominican Republic Licey Tigers had "Verizon" and Verizon's corporate emblem across their backs, while the Lions' backs said "Coca-Cola" in the trademark font. What did commercialism and nationalism add?

The commercialization did not rival the nationalism as four teams, each champion of a nation-state's "winter league" in 2005-06, competed for the Caribbean championship. No one mentioned that Coke won. But the nation was foremost to Álex González after the February 4th game. "This homer is even more important to me than the one I hit for the Marlins in the World Series," he said, referring to a 12th inning game winner in 2003. "This was for my country." Are Mr. González's priorities bad news for his new employers the Boston Red Sox, who signed him earlier that same week? He might have been exaggerating to help promote the Caribbean World Series. But sincere or simply plausible, his comment was probably noticed by the corporate men (they are almost all men) who run Organized Baseball, men called "Lords of the Realm" by John Helyar in his 1994 book on the business history of baseball, and a generation earlier, called "Lords of Baseball" and "Lords of the Game" by Harold Parrott in his book about baseball management. Does it matter whether performances for Major League teams are paramount to the players? The ambivalent staging of the World Baseball Classic suggests that it very much does.

"World Baseball Classic" is a tortured but clever locution. The World Baseball Classic is a tournament gathering national teams from 16 entities, 14 of them nation-states and all represented as "nations" (Puerto Rico has a flag to put on its caps and jackets; "Chinese Taipei" used its Olympic name and flag, not the "Republic of China" flag, not even the name "Taiwan," avoiding trouble with another tournament entry, "China"; the country often called South Korea resolutely self-represented as "Korea"). Not a true world championship, not even a Baseball World Cup, the Lords of the Game insured, just a fun, instant classic tournament. For years the Lords of the Game resisted international competition, mainly by open avoidance. They refused to release players for international tournaments like the Baseball World Cup. Unlike leadership in other professional sports they refused to release players to the Olympics.

But Organized Baseball has now decided to take over international play and establish ways and means on its own terms. The rules for the WBC directly adapt the rule-book of Organized Baseball. They make interesting reading in this regard, occasionally showing the fingerprints of the Lords of the Game behind the curtain of law-like formality: "The role of the 'League President' in the Official Baseball Rules, with respect to the Tournament, shall be performed by the designees of WBCI." WBCI is "World Baseball Classic Incorporated," wholly owned by Major League Baseball (MLB) and the Player's Union. The Classic did not take place after the World Series, like the next rung up a playoff ladder, but rather amidst "Spring Training," the time of exhibition games that do not count for anything. Further, in a formalization of the mode and spirit of spring training games, the WBC put strict limits on pitchers in the tournament, starting pitchers limited to pitch counts well below regular season averages, and appearance limits on relievers. These rules had no parallel in baseball outside of Little League. Many participating nations in the tournament were from the tropics or the southern hemisphere, at the end of their season rather than the beginning, but their best pitchers were not allowed to dominate whole games. This had two competitive benefits for the Lords of the Game. First, it ensured that the World Baseball Classic would not be a no-holds-barred world championship. Second, it played to the strength of the US team, which was expected to be depth, especially in pitching. Also, the US team was set to play every game within the US, the only team with home-field throughout. And the US was guaranteed not to meet most of the Latin American teams. Cuba, the Dominican Republic, Venezuela and the other Latin American teams except Mexico were placed as far from the US team as was possible, never to meet until the very final game (or not at all, as it turned out; Korea, Japan, and Mexico were more than the US could handle).

* * *

So where in this is the capitalism? We start with the last negative dialectic, the denouement "against elementary forms." This is not just about commoditization of baseball. Capitalism is not, merely or mainly, about the commodity as a cultural form. Yes, commodities are important in capitalism, and baseball is a ball game. Roger Angell has written a wonderful piece about the ball, the oblique spheroid, how tightly its movements are controlled in baseball and how, sometimes, it flies free. But to say that capitalism is about commodities and commoditization is roughly as correct as to say that baseball is about the ball and ballization. Commodities are involved. But for all that the commodity form has dominated cultural study of capitalism, and critical social theory since Marx, making the commodity the elementary form of capitalism is a doomed analytic strategy. We cannot actually learn everything about capitalism by way of commodity metaphysics, or by following commodities through circuits of production, exchange and consumption, even if we include all depths of subjectivities connected to commodities and commoditization, with or without commodity fetishism and consciousness true or false. There is simply more involved. More complex things (like WBCI) change the conditions of possibility for commodities, change the structure, build different kinds of commodities and different environments for commodity circulation and consumption.

An awful lot in baseball is not about the ball, though it has implications for the ball, for production, exchange, and use of balls, even fetishization of particular balls. Capitalism is more than turning everything into commodities. The commodity is not even the sure sign of capitalism; as Weber argued, many exchange systems with commodities really shouldn't be called capitalist, if capitalism entails the dynamic features of more recent economic structures. There are ball games that are not baseball.

To clarify, let us examine limits on commoditization in the game. Powerful capitalist institutions often limit processes of commoditization and commodity circulation. Soon, to help me out, I will call in House of Representatives Member George Nethercutt, Republican of Oregon (the guy who beat Tom Foley when the Republicans took over). He will explain the importance of purity, especially for our youth. But we start with the epiphenomenal commoditization in the Caribbean Series. If capitalism is all about commoditizing, then why are the Caribbean Series uniforms more ad-soaked than those of the Major Leaguers? Why, when big money comes to play, are there fewer ads on the players' bodies? Compare with Little League uniforms. To US viewers the Caribbean Series uniforms are more reminiscent of Little League than Major Leagues, though Coca-Cola is not Joe's Hardware. Even the umpire's bodies were rendered into billboards for ads in the cash-challenged Caribbean Series. A DIRECTV logo, complete with blue and white satellite, covered their right shoulders, visible on every pitch to right-handed batters.

The Major Leagues nibble at the edges with ad placement all the time. Outfield walls and other stadium surfaces carry corporate imagery and advertisements, even stadium walls behind the batters. Some are added digitally, visible only in the TV broadcasts. In the age of VCRs and channel surfing, advertisers seek modes of ad placement that cannot be avoided. They pressure Organized Baseball, especially the Major Leagues, for more access for ad placement. An innovation on these lines is purchase of ballpark names. San Diego named its ballpark after sportswriter Jack Murphy in "eternal gratitude" for his efforts to bring Major League baseball to their city, then renamed it Qualcomm Park for cash. They now play in a new stadium, PETCO Park. The Houston Astros bought out of a deal that permanently renamed their stadium "Enron Field" when this began to irritate fans. They now play in the same place, "Minute Maid Park" (a fan writes "I've made three trips to watch the Astros and each time the ballpark has had a different name" at *www.baseballpilgrimages.com*). But Organized Baseball has not gone the way of the Caribbean series, let alone NASCAR auto racing where corporate logos cover the bodies of cars and drivers.

This was tested in 2004. Major League baseball sought to put ads onto the field and the public fought back resoundingly. In May, MLB announced that later that summer, a weekend before the release of the movie *Spiderman 2*, they would excite the enthusiasms of young people by putting spider web designs on the bases and on-deck circles. The fans reacted with such disgust, sportswriters and bloggers with such derision, that Major League Baseball scaled back the next day and cancelled use of webbed bases during any actual games.

It was, to cite another genre, all just a "business decision." When fans and writers protested on the day of the announcement, Baseball Commissioner Bud Selig said, "It isn't worth, frankly, having a debate about." He told an Associated Press reporter on May 6th, 2004 that "I'm a traditionalist. The problem in sports marketing, particularly in baseball, is you're always walking a very sensitive line. Nobody loves tradition and history as much as I do." Tradition versus modernity, distinguished by commoditization, especially advertising: you can analyze the whole situation that way if you want, but not in this book. If it is baseball's traditionalism that keeps ads out then why aren't there ads on NFL gridiron football and NBA basketball uniforms? In Selig's dreams he can sell new kinds of ads as if they are hip new additions to the scene, getting with the times, modernizing a structure in need.

Many fans saw something terrible and impending in the *Spiderman 2* plan, a further commercial infringement into green pastures of the good and pure, in a world with less and less that is clean, decent, wholesome and worthy of love and consumption in one's leisure with one's disposable income. *The Los Angeles Times* of May 7th, 2004 quoted executive director Gary Ruskin of Commercial Alert, a consumer watchdog group that urged fans to boycott the movie and all Sony products, because Sony owned the movie's distributor. "It's time for baseball fans to stand up to the greedy corporations that are insulting us and our national pastime," he said. "How low will baseball sink? Next year, will they replace the bats with long Coke bottles, and the bases with big hamburger buns?" Narrative of a fall, from grace to ads. What grace was that, constituted how?

This is false consciousness of an advertising doom, as if the old ballparks lacked billboards, and all the other baseball institutions began innocent and clean. For a counter-example consider the real history of baseball cards. Long gone are the origins, one side entirely devoted to an advertisement; long gone even is the tobacco, gum, or other commodity they originally accompanied. Baseball cards did not begin amateur and then get seduced by the dark side. They were born as advertising for other commodities, and emerged as a commodity, coming into their own, precisely when they were recognizably salable themselves.

Is capitalism the march of commoditization of everything, billboardization of the body and so on? Not if George Nethercutt has his way, and I want to pause to remember who from what party articulates this aesthetic politics. To Nethercutt it is a cultural struggle, a matter of political will whether we will be overcome by commercialization of our really good things. "Little Leaguers deserve to see their heroes slide into bases, not ads," he wrote to Bud Selig the day of the announcement. A nice turn of phrase, and the little leaguer's imagination is interesting here. The next day, Nethercutt spoke approvingly to *ESPN.com* about the policy reversal. "As commissioner Selig discovered, we baseball fans will put up a fierce fight to protect our national pastime. Thanks to the support of fans today, America's pastime will remain pure tomorrow."

We find ourselves ensconced in a purity and danger story. Champions of the status quo rush to save the future from jeopardy and corruption, and find purity in the game's past. This purity theme resonates with key moments in the game's history. Remember the traumatic Black Sox gambling scandal, a World Series fixed, and the turn to Kenesaw Mountain

Landis and a strong commissionership to protect the game's best interests. Purity was restored by strength. Purity was what Happy Chandler told Cuban team owners that only the US leagues had, while the color line was barely breached, play with Japan banned, and women laughed out of attempting to become players themselves. (This last exclusion has changed little; in April 2006, broadcaster and ex-player Keith Hernandez objected to a woman on the Padre's training staff being present in a Major League dugout.)

What is this purity? It overlaps with what the muscular Christians thought only amateurs could have. How did baseball get it, and how does it keep it, especially in a world that now so threatens the integrity of the World Series? Certainly not by keeping out the influence of money, capital, and all the forces of standardized production and quality control that are hallmarks of highly organized and tightly branded production. In fact, precisely the opposite: the form of purity is a product of standardized production and quality control, marked by exclusive brand names.

The purity of this national pastime, I submit, resembles the purity of a package of Oreos (one of the first, and least changed, products of the National Biscuit Company, i.e. Nabisco). Yes, they are one of the fattiest high calorie things on the market, but a branded object produced with uniformity that guarantees its specific quality. Try selling Oreos stamped with advertisements for something else, and see what happens, or just change the formula of Coke a little, to make it appeal more to Pepsi drinkers. Because it is a game, baseball cannot insure the same uniformity, but it has the promise of much greater excitement. Some games are "good" or even "great." How can greatness be made, its anticipation sold?

The professional turn of baseball leagues began the process of production of a higher quality baseball, evidenced by victories as truly good, worthy of being the measure of other baseball, and increasingly measurable. The structure of leagues and their regular season schedules bring Chadwick's statistics and myriad other numbers into their own, and vice versa. Measurement of excellence becomes possible. Increasingly impressive ballparks are built; multipurpose grandstands (even New York's legendary Polo Grounds) give way to baseball stadiums, the Greek-revival name "stadium" first put on a ballpark by the Yankees. Controlling and elevating the space for the game, and improving fans views of it, embellishing and informing their experience in other ways, all leads forward the complex purity of the game, its real commodiousness. What matters most is what is on the field. Excellence becomes available to experience, visible, with open prospects whose condition of possibility is the structure of the leagues and their championships. Thus, while Nethercutt invokes the purity of youth and the needs of the Little Leaguer above all, actual Little League play of baseball is declining (too stressful, not enough exercise) without undermining the standard of purity in the game. The Major League players do not imagine themselves in Little League, or wish they were playing on a sandlot. It is the other way around: the Major Leagues set the standard. When watching Major League games or even while playing their own games, the Little Leaguers wish themselves worthy of the sport's extreme moments of possibility. They imagine themselves Derek Jeter batting in the World Series, or Curt Schilling pitching with his bloody sock. This kind of purity is not health or innocence or nature. It is a made sublime, capable of being and becoming only in a built environment managed with extreme care and expense. Bakhtin thought that the novel was the most complex of literary genres (Voloshinov thought the scientific treatise was the highest form). Michael Silverstein has been known to argue that language is the pinnacle of all semiotic forms. Baseball is one of the really great games, because so much has been done by so many to organize it, inside of Organized Baseball and outside of it. Its form of purity is a pure product of complexity.

* * *

Does capitalism exploit baseball? One could also argue that baseball exploits capitalism. Capitalism built the environment for almost all the highest forms of baseball that have existed (though Japan went for decades with excellence manifesting mainly in a national school tournament, and the Castro-era Cubans persist with socialist amateurism). Do you need capitalism to have a world championship? No, but it built a good one. Is there still a world championship of baseball, now? The future of the World Series, and with it the structure of excellence in baseball, is at stake.

Comparison of the World Series and the World Baseball Classic will almost always begin and end with the quality of the teams, but there are other issues intrinsic to the structure of play. Who plays who? A sign of the difference of the World Baseball Classic is a novel use of ballplayers' bodies in advertisements. The World Baseball Classic ran elegant advertisements for itself with portions of flags overlain on player's faces, sober expressions against somber backdrops (see Figure 1, page 6). The national emblems made this distinctive. Wrapping the self in the flag is not the same as wrapping the self in advertising. The effect was closer to the opposite, ads announcing that the players in the Classic, soaked in national spirit, were less mercenary, less individual, nobler, possibly even purer, by embodying some higher collective essence. Like the use of uniforms, the flags on uniforms united the players into something more than their mundane selves. But should nations be baseball's higher form of order?

No doubt, the Lords of the Game are ambivalent about how well their World Baseball Classic tournament went. Baseball's COO Robert DuPuy wrote a blog throughout the WBC, effervescent about its quality and excitement (see *bobdupuy.mlblogs.com/bobdupuy*). It probably pleased them that Jake Peavy of the San Diego Padres called his chance to pitch in the tournament "the coolest thing I ever did." After all, he has not been in the World Series yet. They might not even mind that Akinori Otsuka, the relief pitcher who saved the final championship game for Japan, paused and smiled when I asked him (through the official translator) whether he would rather help Japan win again in the next World Baseball Classic, in 2009, or help his Texas Rangers win the World Series. "You don't have to answer," the translator told him (in English), and then he said, in English, "both." WBC advertising declared these games special because, one player after another said, "We'll be there for our country. Will you be there for yours?" But a good thing can go too far. If the Lords of the Game had merely meant to wrap themselves in the flag, in the disingenuous sense of the aphorism — what they do playing the anthem before games, and with red-white-and-blue bunting for Opening Day and the World Series — they might now find it hard to get the purity of their extant world championship back from the world of flags and nations. I doubt they were pleased when, after the WBC, columnist William Rhoden wrote in *The New York Times* that MLB cannot call its championship the World Series, that it has to call it something else.

* * *

The first "real" or "modern" World Series was not the first World Series. The 1903 series between the National League champion Pittsburgh Pirates and the American League champion Boston Red Sox was called "the World's Championship Series" by its promoters and by the influential annual baseball guides published by Spalding and by Reach. But the *Spalding Guide*, in particular, had been recording "World's Championship" results already for decades. First was an 1887 postseason series between Chicago, champion of the National League, and St. Louis, champion of the American Association (as I learn from "Origin of the Name 'World Series'" by Doug Pappas, in the SABR newsletter *Outside the Lines* Fall 2001). This title "World Series" was born of a desire to hype the sale of sporting goods, and of deliberate irony and insouciance. The 1887 *Spalding Guide* editor gently ridiculed the pretensions of the two leading professional leagues. Since the leagues "both entitle their championship contests each season as those for the base ball championship of the United States," a more grandiose name was required for the meeting between them. By 1890, though, the guide had made the name a regular title for such series.

Before the World Series became the contest between NL and AL champions, the World Series idea was the idea of pinnacle championship, ultimate baseball. The chance to stage such a championship — lost if the new American League drew off players and went its own way — was one reason why the two leagues agreed to recognize each other as "major" and form one National Agreement in 1903. (Shades of the 2006 Yankees, the 1904 Giants didn't like it; some National League broadcasters still seem to resent the accommodation, calling theirs the "senior circuit," the American League the "junior circuit.") The name was shortened from "World's Championship Series" to "World's Series" in the *Reach Guide* in 1912, and first to "World Series" in the *Spalding Guide* in 1918. *The Sporting News* in its annual guide used "World's Series" through 1963.

So the actual World Series is not owned by the actual world. It is not even owned by "baseball" or what we might term "the world of baseball," a universe of interactions among all recognizing the game and its meanings, value and practices. It is not owned by any set of stakeholders, but rather by specific shareholders, the owners of the Major League franchises. And, the key point so far, these shareholders never lost control of this World Series or even any Baseball World to the stakeholders. The shareholders brought the stakeholders into being, built the environment so attractive to the attention and imaginaries of the paying fans, whose future of purity and right to continue paying for it Representative Nethercutt so adroitly champions. Nothing prevented amateur clubs or play, which still go on, but to invoke one of Latour's insights, this is an instance where something new came into being where nothing had been before, in a way that changed the place of everything else. Something good was created. A commodity came into circulation that created its own audience, something in Martha Kaplan's felicitous phrase "neither traditional nor foreign," constituting its own use value by adding to the world. How?

* * *

Next section we turn to Max Weber, and in the one after to Thorstein Veblen, to help answer that question: how capitalism creates and controls particular new use values, what will start as a problem in reason and practical culture, and continue via Veblen's theory of the nature of the firm. Here, we end with a coda on the commodity.

The idea of "capitalism," an –ism that is a whole system, came well after the development of a

capitalist mode of production (as historian Dennis
Wrong has argued). This is not unique. The idea of a
"revolution" developed mostly after the French had
theirs, as Keith Baker has shown. Keith Tribe has
shown that the idea of "industry" in the sense of a
large-scale division of labor organized by investment,
rather than "industry" as strenuous activity of an individual, came late in the nineteenth century, long after
the "industrial revolution" (let alone the first large
scale European colonial industrial enterprises, and
large scale manufacturing in the Old World preceding
European capitalism). Concepts that elegantly organize complex facts, concepts that make description
possible (one of Weber's phrases), often come late in
the history of complex activity. The understanding
they can provide can in turn have its own effects. Marx
felt this way about "the commodity." He made it the
first topic in *Capital* because he believed that political
economy post festum had mistaken it, an historical
artifact, for a thing of nature, and thereby misunderstood economic history. To clarify for readers interested in Marx, I think Marx also misunderstood some
dimensions of use value. Jean Baudrillard and Marshall
Sahlins have each made major contributions to the
reconsideration of use value — see especially
Baudrillard's *For a Critique of the Political Economy of the
Sign* and Sahlins' *Culture and Practical Reason*. While
Baudrillard tried to constitute a capitalism characterized by tyranny of a code of signs, and proposed that
utilitarian and even symbolic use values were now,
along with exchange value, dominated by a third kind
of value, sign value, Sahlins, more reasonably,

suggested that Marx neglected the complexity of meaning in use value, tending to accept a utilitarian vision of use, as if uses of things came by nature, despite Marx's skepticism of utilitarian accounts of the origins and history of exchange values. Sahlins shows that real attention of use value leads ineluctably to culture.

What then are these complex cultural phenomena, like baseball, in Kaplan's phrase "neither traditional nor foreign"? We could ignore the problem and take at face value that baseball was always already traditional, because it keeps saying that it is. That is good enough for Bud Selig. But here we have Selig, the man more traditional than anyone, or so he told us, installing a massive new international tournament. Can we spot any other commodities in this class, things unprecedented, things never before known, valuable new things that change the map when they emerge? Yes, and they have a category all their own. They are just about everywhere, in the top-this, creatively competitive mercantile history of luxury. Baseball's traditionalism is part of its cachet.

Historians of capitalism tend to treat the mercantile history of long distance high-end commerce in luxuries as prehistoric to a transformation of the real economy on capitalist terms. Marx defines commodities materially first, as things with an objective use, and more than that, things that are needed. Fake natural utility is his heuristic starting point. But the actual history of the word and idea of "commodity" reveals its own complex composition as a genre of things. "Commodity" does not begin as the name of a class of things available for purchase that meet definite needs. Rather, as one might glean from the term commode, it also, especially in its "obsolete" meanings, refers to commodious character to a thing, preferential alternative provided by the commodity to what one might do for one's self, the state of preferability or luxury of a person or thing. An old definition of quality in architecture is "commodity, fitness, and price," a formulation that precisely separates the commodity of a thing from its fitness or utility to a purpose, and its cost. Similarly, consider a particularly clear instance of use from the *Oxford English Dictionary*, "1612 BREREWOOD Lang. & Relig. xiii. 141 Not to be taken as a rule of necessity..but..rather.. as a rule of commodity." I recommend a look at the *OED* and particularly its usage date chart for "commodity." Not until the seventeenth century does usage begin with the sense "anything that one trades or deals in." Earlier usage is dominated by senses of quality or condition of persons or things.

Thus everything in the word fits with the European mercantile history narrated by Fernand Braudel: commodity is the key feature of goods for large scale mercantile long distance dealers in luxury, who only found reasons in the most recent centuries to become investors in production of more and more kinds of "commodity." The history of capitalism, as a history of commoditization in this sense, could be written as the transformation of increasing numbers of things into luxuries one can have only if one can afford them, including shelter, food, sometimes even water or air (which would explain in a nutshell why solving problems of poverty never spontaneously emerge from the operations of capitalists). But, if such a perspective explains a wish to rise up and defend those Little Leaguers' rights (to what? not their own second base free of ads, nor ads off their own backs, not food for their families, no, something about their heroes' second bases, the commodity of the game they watch) let us consider a list of the things that did not simply, naturally, or spontaneously fold out of the concept of the commodity itself, even if we leave aside the historical vicissitudes of that complex concept.

Capitalism has also included taxes, accounting, mortgages, banks, slavery, indentured labor, state issued currencies, insurance, stocks, bonds, and many other species of financial instrument and mechanisms for their exchange, a plethora of creative forms of contract as well as various regulatory institutions for their enforcement and mediation. Cultural study of capitalism that requires the commodity to reveal all secrets will never, I submit, get you to appreciate the significance of all these kinds of capitalist things, these genres of capitalist institution. Nor above all will it explain the colonially-emergent institution which I would rate the most important in the actual recent centuries of capitalism: joint stock companies, corporations, the firm. Perhaps these three names do not refer simply and entirely to the same thing from different perspectives, historical, contemporary, and apologetic. There might be use for fine distinctions. But it is time a critical anthropology and history of capitalism dwelt less on dialectics of commodity and subjectivity, and looked harder for locations within which capitalists — split fatefully between owners and management — make and remake capitalist worlds. For reasons intrinsic to its mission in myriad ways, anthropology has always investigated the history of labor and work, and treated management as the other, as if management is the party of the second part, which it never is (especially in Veblen's new order). But what does a critical anthropology of management look at? Management, licensed by structure to be responsible first of all to ownership, mandated in fact to be ruthless and creative in all dealings with everyone else, working and more recently playing with other people's money, what does it do? What differences does it make, in what worlds?

Can we connect how baseball came to create itself, make its own audience, add value or commodity to its game, how the world of baseball grew from New York clubs to a century of World Series, can we connect this history to the history of its incorporation, the modes of its organization and reorganization, especially by owners and investors?

Management of a Game:
Branch Rickey and Max Weber

Let's begin with two views of Branch Rickey, the St. Louis Cardinals' General Manager. The first is a quotation from player Pepper Martin recalling his first Cardinals World Series and the second describes Rickey at his first World Series in 1926, both from Peter Golenbock's *The Spirit of St. Louis*:

> Mr. Heydler, the league president, talked to us first; then Mr. John McGraw spoke; but then came Mr. Branch Rickey. His theme was: The greatest attribute of a winning ballplayer is a desire to win that dominates! I have never forgotten those words.

He brought every single Cardinal off his seat with an address that beat anything I ever heard. He reminded us that we had dreamed of this moment from boyhood. We had schemed and scratched and fought and gone hungry to get here, and here we were, and what in heaven's name were we going to do about it?

Well, we rushed out of there cheering, and I personally got down on my knees in front of our dugout and I kissed the ground, and I actually prayed to God to help me have the desire to win that dominates. And I meant every word I prayed. I really did.

During the World Series, Branch Rickey was visiting a friend, Gene Mudd. When the Cards won the final game, Rickey told Mudd, "Gene, you can't possibly realize what this means to me... to the club. Not only vindication of all I've dreamed of and fought for, but it means capital to reinvest and spend for expansion and scouting and large training camps and more teams for developing the finest players."

Victory: end or means for Mr. Rickey? End or means, or both?

* * *

Revolutionary advancements in management are storied parts of baseball and business history more generally. Keeping with complexity, we turn to transformations in the midst of baseball management history, not its beginnings. Many good histories of labor relations track the emergence of baseball's antitrust exemption and the rise and fall of the notorious "reserve clause," the legal device that bound players to the first contract they signed with a team in Organized Baseball. We will jump, instead, to Branch Rickey's first major innovation.

A recent management controversy in baseball follows from *Moneyball*, business writer Michael Lewis's portrayal of Billy Beane, Oakland Athletics general manager. The conceit of *Moneyball*, and apparently of Beane, is that Beane is baseball's first executive to use rational rather than traditional techniques to evaluate and deploy talent. In Lewis's feel-good narrative, reason is the hero against otherwise overwhelming forces of endlessly greedy big-market teams. According to Lewis, reason is intrinsically reductionistic. For example, on-base percentage slides gradually from an important measure of offensive talent to a principal measure to the only rational measure, on naïve grounds that teams with more baserunners score more. (As if, for minimal counter-examples, opposing teams won't throw more strikes when batters work for walks, and combat slow runners with ground-ball pitching to get double plays.) Scouts are presented as passionate creatures who fall in love with certain skills and body types, over-anticipating success for some players and neglecting others.

In *Three Nights in August*, describing games between rivals St. Louis Cardinals and Chicago Cubs, journalist Buzz Bissinger opens the lifeworld of Cardinals manager Tony La Russa. As "manager," La Russa decides who plays when, on the field in the team uniform every day; in Bissinger's narrative the Cardinals general manager, negotiatior of contracts and rosters, figures rarely. Bissinger presents his book as a defense of the baseball insiders against Lewis's claims, evidence of the power of old-fashioned knowledge and craft against Lewis's heroes, the thirtysomething MBA types in "the front office" who treat "the manager as middle manager" and turn baseball toward cold calculations.

These two choices — reason as reduction to oversimplified models, versus intuition and wisdom embodied in insider craft steeped in tradition — are not our only options. A far more capacious approach to reason in relation to institutions, values and worldviews is available in Max Weber's sociology, with particular relevance to "revolutions" in the management of investments. For insights into capitalism, and baseball history, we turn next to Weber and Rickey.

The anti-trust exemption and the reserve clause would not escape Weber's notice when assessing the capital investment and its management in baseball. In his extensive writings on economy and society, Weber emphasized the legal preconditions above all factors in the development of markets and an investment driven economy. Most students, handed Weber's *Protestant Ethic and the Spirit of Capitalism* as an antidote to Marx since early in the Cold War, are led away from the larger issues in Weber's sociology of capitalism. That essay, in quest of a reason why capitalism developed (he thought) in Europe, and out to illustrate that religious worldviews can be economically relevant (and thus that a separated and totalized science of economics, Marxian or otherwise, will always be flawed), pleas in the end against one-sided approaches to complex phenomena. It is a plea not to be ignored, for all that it usually is. Weber would have been interested in muscular Christianity and in baseball's quasi-religious imagery, shrines and heroes, but more interested in the risks and opportunities created by another built environment, the market for players and its structure in contract law.

As Weber discusses it, rationality is about means and ends. Ends can come from cultures, religions, and free inventions, from conscious, acute deliberations or unconsciously sedimenting habits, always with aesthetic and affective dimensions, matters of meaning. Means are things necessary and useful, the tools, materials, plans and techniques, used to realize the ends of action. Two points Weber stresses about means are that means can influence orientation to ends — notoriously, money, an ultimately fungible means, can become an end in itself — and that effective means sediment in history, changing conditions of possibility for action. But unlike his dialectical countrymen, Weber does not see a generalized dialectic between means and ends at work. Not everything that can be done will be done, feeding the poor the classic example. Senses of what should be done have an actual, irreducible history that is only partly explicable by the history of what could be done. Weber is an historical realist, closer methodologically to Clausewitz than to Marx or Hegel on the roads out of Kantian idealism.

Capitalism is, at core, pursuit of profit? Ruthless pursuit of profit, detached from all traditions or sentiments? Weber scorned such propositions. Pursuit of profit in exchange and mercantile ruthlessness were parts of all or most of human history, he thought. Weber believed that the dynamics of capitalist business enterprises actually required the tempering of pursuit of profit, especially if that "end in itself" was tantamount to acquisitiveness, desire for wealth or property. Weber was more interested in factors leading to sustained investments, self-reproducing institutionalizations of productive capital. He tended to diagram capitalist history from the vantage of decisions of investors (a partial view of the issues at best) and he would likely look at baseball history that way: under what circumstances would financiers fund baseball's would-be captains of industry? To do what, and why?

Among other things Weber is a pioneer of the sociology of risk. Histories of the formal techniques for risk assessment such as Bernstein's *Against the Gods* ignore Weber (and before him Clausewitz, an obvious master of substantive risk assessment) but there is much to be gained from Weber's economic sociology to reconsider real risk, to avoid merely reducing it to formal models of game. Clausewitz warned that in war, formal models would get you killed. Weber just thought they would limit you, especially to the degree that you mistook them for reality. History, to both Clausewitz and Weber, was constituted in large part by the friction between reality and our conceptions of it, since our conceptions would never adequately cover the whole of reality and its parts; Weber added also that a surplus developed on the side of our conceptions and their consequences, that unintended consequences of intentional actions were a major part of real social history.

When would the holders of significant, fungible capital risk investing it in enterprises under the management of others, rather than holding it themselves in the form of property that either held its value durably, or could reproduce itself with minimized reliance on outside markets (as in a plantation, estate or oikos)? When would holders of capital invest in production of commodities for a market, relying on markets to provide them with both all the necessary means and all the necessary outlets for their product? When would a baseball team stock its roster with players from its own minor league teams or even baseball "academies" or plantations that it owns and runs for this purpose? When would it rely on markets to deliver players, just as it relies on markets to deliver ticket-buying fans? We will contrast Weber's probing approach to these problems with the Nobel-winning, panglossian plain tales of Ronald Coase. But first we will review an actual revolution in baseball management worked by Branch Rickey.

Branch Rickey is in the Hall of Fame, famous principally for bringing Jackie Robinson and other black players into the Major Leagues, breaking the color barrier. (I have written in some detail recently about Rickey, Robinson, the color barrier, the nation, and world baseball, in the *International Journal of the History of Sport*.) But while Rickey saw breaking Organized Baseball's color barrier as his major achievement in life, it was not his first significant innovation with massive ramifications for Organized Baseball.

While General Manager of the St. Louis

Cardinals, from 1919 to 1942, Branch Rickey developed what he called the "farm system." His Cardinals arranged "working agreements" with teams in other leagues within Organized Baseball, sometimes part ownership and increasingly, controlling ownership shares, whenever and wherever he could afford it and arrange it. He stocked them like fishponds with players he could "call up" when needed, without further negotiation over contracts. The contracts behind the scheme ranged from unwritten "gentlemen's agreements," to secret but formal arrangements, and eventually became open and absolute contractual matters. Especially for teams that his Cardinals wholly owned, Rickey arranged things so that the Major League team paid all the players and held all their contracts, and retained the power to arrange and rearrange not only rosters but even plans for playing time, with an eye above all on player development for eventual Major League play. This was a new deal for minor league baseball teams, which theretofore had mainly made their books balance by selling the most valuable players they held under contract at the end of each season. And this new deal was particularly popular during the great depression in the 1930s, when many minor league teams otherwise went bankrupt, and whole leagues disappeared. To establish his system, Rickey not only needed to finance it, but also to face down resistance from minor league officials protecting the integrity (i.e. commodity, in the original sense) of their leagues. He had to overcome fierce resistance from commissioner Kenesaw Mountain Landis, who conveniently ignored the general implications of the reserve clause when he accused Rickey in particular of running "chain gangs."

How and why did Rickey build the farm system? What conditions of possibility enabled his "genius" to express itself so effectively?

No doubt, as Golenbock put it, "Vision was part of Branch Rickey's genius," and that "What he foresaw often came to fruition." The Jackie Robinson literature includes more heated debate about Rickey's larger motives, but the farm system history provides ample material. Was Rickey out to make improvements where they should be made, on a mission to improve the world? (A tea-totaling Methodist who favored prohibition, Rickey said he was.) Was Rickey just out to win baseball games (as some critics of his color line work alleged; was Jackie used?) or "worse," was he just out to use baseball to make money (as Dizzie Dean realized that Rickey certainly did, the first time Dean dropped by Rickey's home to ask to borrow some)? I am against any desire to frame Rickey's motives in a single, simple (game-like) framework. All three and more are real parts of his motives and action.

Most histories of Rickey's invention of the farm system start in the same place: he did not do what was expected of him when he became the St. Louis General Manager in 1919. The New York Giants, the dominant team in the National League, wanted the new General Manager of nearly bankrupt St. Louis to sell them its best player, Rogers Hornsby. Selling players was a principal modality of baseball business then, and still happens now: poorer teams sold players to balance the books. The reserve clause enabled the practice, another of its virtues for the owners. (Hollywood also tied up its talent with option clauses, but never managed a right to trade it or farm out the options. Between Rickey's time and ours, the Players Union has obtained rights to controlled "free agency" at specific moments in a career, and has won much higher incomes for players, after forcing a court to notice that the "reserve clause" could not possibly actually be legal in the US.) Rickey resisted settling St. Louis into the routines of financially weak teams, selling veterans to stronger clubs or trading them for younger players. He financed ownership of minor league teams every way he could, starting with a windfall when the Cardinals abandoned their decrepit stadium and sold the land under it, becoming tenants instead at the park of the St. Louis Browns.

Rickey's strategy worked as a confluence of the interests he served. He wanted to win (Pepper Martin's recollection above suggests his charisma there) and he wanted a large capital to reinvest, World Series victory becoming mere means to a growing, consolidating network of player development investments. He wanted more players in development, more scouting try-outs, more minor league teams. His minor league operations financed themselves by selling young talent that he did not fully respect or need to other organizations, while keeping the players he thought most talented. By 1925, Golenbock summarizes, the Cardinals "owned or controlled teams at every minor league level from Class D to Triple A. On a chalkboard in Rickey's office was a list of every player in the organization. Rickey kept track of the status of every one of them."

If this is about money, it is not just about Rickey's own income. The corporate aesthetics of Rickey's dream, as a whole plan, drive all the particular pieces in coordination. Weber, famously, worried that advanced capitalism would become an iron cage, a machinery ineluctably disenchanted. But Rickey seems particularly enchanted, as passionate about player development and team improvement as, say, the Yankee's owner George Steinbrenner is about championships. (Steinbrenner was once asked when he will win enough World Series, and answered "never.") And what enchanted Rickey was the power of his organization to generate better baseball and better baseball players.

Management of a game, or an enterprise treated like a game, can be an enchanting business, especially to some personalities (as Ruth Benedict already warned us; see the second preface). Genius Rickey defied the ordinary rules and tried a fundamentally new strategy. But why, under conditions of advanced capitalism, was his new strategy verging on autarkic? Why did genius choose increasingly controlled and contained labor, averse to dependence on markets to buy or trade for players?

For all Marx's ridicule of Adam Smith, Marx did not doubt the importance of free labor. Marx treated the topic ironically. Free labor was labor free from all access to means of production and subsistence. But Marx thought the emergence of a proletariat of leveled, free wage labor was quintessential to advanced development of the capitalist mode of production. Weber also saw free labor as the quintessential means of rational capitalism, since its flexibility provided such utility to capital. Why then was free labor not the basis of Organized Baseball?

Yes, the players are free to go, just not free to play elsewhere in Organized Baseball. Thus they weren't really slaves, or prisoners on "chain gangs," pace Landis or Harry Edwards. But it is still fair to compare the contemporary baseball "academies" of the Caribbean to plantations. They are industrially organized sites of production of capitalist commodities; the crop they grow is professional baseball players. The players aren't slaves or even indentured. The pathos of the "academies" in Venezuela or the Dominican Republic is that the barbed wire surrounding the fields is there to keep other young men out. (For details see Rob Ruck's *The Tropic of Baseball* and Alan Klein's *Sugarball*.)

Against Rickey, Landis defended purity of minor league competition, teams of players devoted only to winning there, contracts sacrosanct. The farm system revolution in Organized Baseball enthralled the rest of the league structure to the service of the pinnacle. It made development of Major League players the highest priority of the minor leagues. The crucial National Agreement of 1903 tried to balance the rights of players to develop and earn a living, the property rights of investors running clubs as businesses, and the spirit of competition in each league. Despite strenuous efforts to prevent change, Rickey like the Red Stockings fifty years earlier proved an irresistible competitive force. He won games and made money. As a result, Rickey provoked a vertical integration of relations once regulated by markets. His system better mitigated risks, not only because it controlled talent (as did Hollywood, when it could) but because it developed it.

Rickey's vertical integration proved an irresistible force also in the charismatic sense. The other teams all went out and built farm systems, of varying extent, of their own. Rickey's success produced a kind of tulipomania for baseball player farming among MLB organizations, and by 1949 there were 59 active minor leagues, most with most or all teams affiliated with Major League organizations. But the greatest competitive advantage was in fact gained by the Cardinals when they had Rickey's elaborate and monitored farm system, well beyond what anyone else had. Rickey pursued vertical integration for competitive advantage in part because of the market situation of the poorer club that he ran. The buying of players was just too expensive and involved too much friction when a less well funded club sought to solve roster problems as they emerged. Notoriously in baseball, the organizations in competition raise their prices for brethren in obvious need. When your third baseman is suddenly injured, it becomes much harder to buy or trade for the best one on the market. Beyond mere scarcity, real strategies of others made relying on the market risky. And Rickey was even able to exploit its scarcities by selling his farm system surpluses. He also, clearly, loved his business of talent evaluation and player development. He devoted his life to baseball.

* * *

Ronald Coase's theory of the nature of the firm rescued, for neo-classical economics, the existence of firms or corporations as rational entities, by discovering a reason intrinsic to them acceptable to "market fundamentalists" (to borrow a phrase from George Soros). Markets always come first, and the problem of the existence of firms is depicted as the problem of why a rational manager would rely on employees rather than markets. State planning and private firms are taking over what already exists, integrated by the price mechanism of markets, and are successful to the extent that they lower costs, since there are a variety of costs involved in market transactions. Thus marginalist analysis implies that an equilibrium will always be found between planning structures and integration by price mechanism, especially since, as Coase says in *The Nature of the Firm*, "businessmen will be constantly experimenting, controlling more or less" and "firms arise voluntarily because they represent a more efficient method of organizing production." The rise of the firm, as Coase imagines it, is always a movement from many pre-existing contracts to a controlling structure, "For this series of contracts is substituted one."

This imaginary fits poorly the situations that were precisely the actual origin of firms, as when banks gave mortgages to planters, or stock markets funded companies of young agents, prepared to cut plantations into captured wilderness for tropical commodities, sugar, spices, tobacco, tea, chocolate, opium, usually employing labor moved long distances and disciplined by direct violence. There is more in the universe than in Coase's imagination, more motives for the controlling powers of firms than their cost efficiencies. Companies made possible enterprises that would otherwise have been too risky, and created systems of commodity production ex nihilo, or else at unprecedented volumes and scales. Firms were built like engines to deliver profits on vectors towards their owners, and generated unprecedented outputs, out of locations Europeans took and controlled by force. They made production possible in even in locations not previously the site of markets in the commodities produced, and locations lacking labor markets. And semi-autarkic grand design was part of the European plantation system everywhere it went, the first European industrial revolution. Even when local labor was available for sale and cheap, plantations commonly underutilized it in favor of more expensive slaves and indentured labor.

But twentieth century baseball already had developed player markets, and a structure of competition between clubs. So why this turn to farm systems, and why then? Coase is certainly right that businesses experiment. But note that the actual history of Organized Baseball was not many contracts being replaced by one, but many contracts fostered by one big one, the reserve clause. Baseball's legally sustained anti-trust status and its ability to allocate players and keep their salaries low was the foundation for both Major and minor leagues. Rickey was renovating. Baseball's system was already all too organized, and organized against his Cardinals — information was all too public about needs and strategies, and all too efficient a system of player movements, by way of the player markets regulated by the National Agreement, enabled the rich teams to get richer. Something more autarkic was the solution, precisely, for a club that an actually existing market was fully prepared to kneecap, over and over and over.

A Weberian definition of the issues and options can be elegantly opposed to Coase's precisely because Weber was aware of the historical, constructed nature of market operations, and above all their legal preconditions. The law itself, Weber thought, in the sense of a system of predictable enforcement of contracts, was a necessity for anyone intending to rely on contracts, especially complicated ones. Without confidence in enforcement the risk was intolerable. Coase wrote of risk perceptions and preferences, but Weber looks squarely at risk reality and the social engineering that changes realities of risk. Capital always pushes law toward formally rationalized, precedent based adjudication, away from substantive rationality, especially away from respect for justice, precisely because, as he argues in *General Economic History*, "it relies upon a law that can be counted upon, like a machine." And formal rationalization, in turn, renders substantively uneven terrain inevitable, not least since the highly technical rendering of judgments makes legal intervention itself expensive and the courts another tool of the powerful. The utility of markets was historically variable, and dependent on legal structures and forces.

In 1919, the year Rickey began to build his farm system, the National Association of Professional

Baseball Leagues, i.e. the consortium of the minor leagues, repudiated its National Agreement with the two Major Leagues. They could see leagues outside of Organized Baseball, notably the robust Pacific Coast League, obtaining much higher prices for potential star players than were allowed under the rules of the reigning National Agreement, which established a draft and set prices for all player contracts. The leagues of the NAPBL sought relief from the contract that held down their own player costs, because it held down their profits on player sales equally. Predictably there was hell down their road when they all sought new profits in player exchanges mostly with each other. Branch Rickey was in the right place, at the right time, to offer something for nothing, good players already being paid, even co-ownership investments, and more players in future where those came from, in exchange for, eventually, everything.

Other factors for the demise of minor league independence are commonly cited. Rickey suspected that TV damaged attendance; perhaps it did orient people more toward metropolitan teams. Other sports and leisure industries did rise. Somewhat more obscurely, Rickey himself blamed the automobile, pleasant drives as an alternative leisure activity, neglecting the convenience they afforded fans attending games. But obviously, fan morale was hurt by management's transparent willingness to move players for reasons little connected to competitiveness in any league short of the pinnacle. In Coase's just-so story, the efficiency has only one measure and no vectors. It is simply monetary cost. In baseball, structures that are efficient in some dimensions and toward some ends harm other interests and prospects. Minor league gate (like Coca Cola bottler's profits) might be deliberately sacrificed to streamline other efficiencies (like Coca Cola's profits). The engineering of complex chains of transactions is a specialty with far more to monitor than mere transaction costs. Weber's capitalists, like Braudel's, were considerably more predatory, precisely not in a natural or inevitable order of things, but rather, responsive to real institutions often built for other reasons.

The approaches of Weber and Coase also share similarities. Both resolutely analyze from the perspective of the capitalist agent, and study allocation and transaction decisions from the middle out and the top down. Both render the history of institutions as a history of enacted concepts and models in real world trials of strength, some kind of natural or social history of reason. I want to put the World Baseball Classic into a history of innovative reason and its consequences. But I also want to do more, to go farther into its politics, and its place in the cultural history of the politics of the firm, its place in the extension of American games.

Before we consider the commercial and competitive logic of the World Baseball Classic, we will look at another of baseball's structural crises, the one that had Happy Chandler down in Cuba, Organized Baseball's reckoning with the era of decolonization. And we could use more help with the theory of the firm than Weber can give us, precisely because he expects management always to be reasonable.

Happy, Veblenesque
Baseball and Decolonization

> It can't be a World Series unless your champion
> plays our Mexican pennant winner. You know, we
> also are in the world.
>
> —Jorge Pasquel,
> quoted in David Pietrusza, *Major Leagues*

> Sabotage is the beginning of wisdom in industrial
> business.
> —Thorstein Veblen, *Absentee Ownership*

Kenesaw Mountain Landis finally gave up his position
at the commanding heights of Organized Baseball, by
dying on November 25, 1944. Organized Baseball

considered as a firm had serious problems and multiple opportunities. Commissioner Landis had fought but failed to prevent wholesale reorganization of the minor leagues into farm system properties. In the process, the powers of his office were gradually trimmed. During the world war, organizations with strong farms could replace men off to war, while at the other extreme, the cheapskate likes of Clark Griffith resorted to "ivory hunting," sending scouts in Cuba to find white-looking players to sign for low wages. Griffith's Senators had eleven Cubans on their 1944 roster, not all particularly good players. The team finished last. It survived financially only because rent was paid for Griffith Stadium (there's a pure, traditional stadium name for you) by a successful professional baseball team, the Homestead Grays of the Negro Leagues. Observers in Washington had to wonder which local team was better — but few regularly attended the games of both. Urban demographic change, the great migration north of African-Americans, had surrounded Griffith Stadium with an African-American neighborhood, Organized Baseball's "problem" in many cities. Change was coming.

The end of war brought a flood of players back, heroes who might or might not still be skilled at baseball. It remained to be seen, and planned, what the bigger picture of Pax Americana, American political power in a new world order, would mean for Organized Baseball. Vision guys like Rickey would soon negotiate and even conspire with African-American journalists like Wendell Smith and players like Robinson, John Wright, and others. Landis, in one of his last significant acts, had prevented maverick Bill

Veeck from breaking the color barrier in 1944. Veeck eventually broke the American League color line in 1947, signing slugger Larry Doby of the Newark Eagles as soon as he owned the Cleveland Indians. Veeck wanted as early as 1942 to buy the bankrupt Philadelphia Phillies and win the pennant with a full team of Negro League stars. Landis sabotaged the plan, blocking the sale and eventually arranging sale of the team to others, for less money and with lesser dreams.

Other pressures were building when Landis died. Every one of the Major League franchises was located north of the Mason-Dixon line and no farther west than St. Louis. But the increasing and visible hierarchy of leagues made cities with only minor league teams feel minor league themselves. The proud and often profitable Pacific Coast League had never yet accepted a rank in Organized Baseball, and was beginning to discuss Major status for itself. PCL veteran Lefty O'Doul, one of its legendary players and successful managers, reopened relations with Japanese baseball after the war. He visited Japan in 1946, led a 1949 tour by his San Francisco Seals team, and a 1951 Major League tour. O'Doul had fond memories of 1930s Major League baseball tours and visits to Japan. When Landis banned play with the Japanese in 1935, the Pacific Coast teams were not affected. During the 1936 Tokyo Giants tour of the US, O'Doul's Seals learned how well the Japanese team could play, losing to them twice.

But Happy Chandler's immediate international challenge was not from Japan, nor the Pacific Coast. It

came from Latin American baseball. The Mexican
League tried to become Major in the late 1940s, and
Happy Chandler prevented it. Here we look more
closely at what happened. This is not a story of
empire, but of other kinds of exercise of power. Long
before the 1940s, the US had set its southern border,
and would not include more Mexicans into the frame-
works of cherished US social and political institutions.
This is a story of keeping outsiders down and out.

How do firms actually respond to threats and
opportunities? To dreams of commodity, and straight
tales of reason in action, Thorstein Veblen provides an
alternative conceptual vocabulary for measuring and
modeling corporate organization and planning: vested
interest, collusion, surveillance, jealousy, obstruction
and deflection, expediency, restraint of trade, and
sabotage.

* * *

The British East India Company was a leading
early joint stock company. The first markets for stock
in company enterprises, in Amsterdam and London,
were originally dominated by colonial and maritime
enterprises, and above all by the old world trading
companies, especially the Dutch and British East India
Companies. Joint stock companies, bodies politic and
corporate, were instituted as partners in sovereignty,
trading profits and shares for monopoly patents with
royal houses that would otherwise have to rely on
elected parliaments for funds they wanted for armies
and war with each other. Weber was not surprised that
companies, these signature capitalist institutions, were

born of and for colonial purposes. He understood that they needed to partake of military and sovereign power in their early days, to enforce their own contract law as they went, and thus were precisely suited to be extensions of sovereign monopoly under colonial conditions for commercial purposes. They made investments possible that would otherwise be too risky. Weber simply did not understand that these colonial institutions, these joint stock companies, were to become the predominant economic form for future global capitalism. For this, we need to turn to Thorstein Veblen.

In a fragment on markets, which can be found in *Economy and Society*, Weber once wrote that market relationships are the most impersonal possible human relations; citing Sombart and sounding a bit like Simmel, too, Weber romanticized the dehumanization of complete objectification of trading partners and the limited interest taken in others when the whole orientation is to "the commodity and only to that," a wholly "rational, purposeful pursuit of interests." Weber argued that "The market community as such is the most impersonal relationship of practical life into which humans can enter with each other" and that "Such absolute depersonalization is contrary to all the elementary forms of human relationship." Several things are wrong with this argument. It affiliated with affect, versus reason, every value other than material gain, including the "person," the "community," and all the rest of human culture, rather than deploying Weber's own method to delineate different ends and means pursued rationally. It also underestimated the

capacity of reasoning to constitute instrumental relationships that render other people into faceless means,
far more absolute depersonalizations than mere
market exchanges. Orlando Patterson in *Slavery and
Social Death* analyzes another extreme, refusal to
recognize a person owned as a thing. A third mode of
planned and executed disregard, the one in corporate
structures, is possible only in social distances constituted by complexity.

Complexity, the management of long chains of
interaction and transaction, actually enables far more
possibilities. Weber's fragment on markets suggests
that he never really attended to the basic moral structure of the firm, the joint stock company, and the
modern corporation, starting with the human relationship between the so-called stockholders and the so-
called stakeholders. In a relationship only fully explicable when one locates the first flowering of joint stock
companies in colonial relationships, the owners of
companies hire employees to actually contract with
workers and customers. Those employees are not
merely, like Weber's most alienated humans, out to
minimize what they give for what they get, here on
their masters' behalf, or like Patterson's owners deny-
ing the existence of social relationship. These new
employees, these managers, are actually required to
develop and sustain networks of exchange which
extract the largest and most routine profits possible, in
the ongoing reckoning of the sum of their exchanges
with labor and customers. If alienation of various
kinds is the signature of the subjectivity of market
exchange, of slavery and of selling one's own labor,

what do we title the active, routinized extraction that is intrinsic to management, this license and duty to manipulate stakeholders, the people you deal with, on behalf of intangible, absent shareholders? How do we understand the social system that emerged when this institution, the colonial trading company, brought home this institutional structure and taught the power of joint-stock organization to other capitalist enterprises? An English world, "business," was retooled to define the new moral realm, the realm that this century has been infused with the logic of games. Again, the *OED* date chart tracks changing usage. Obsolete now is "business" as the state or quality of being busy, a use that thrived from the fourteenth to seventeenth centuries. Meanwhile, "that about which one is busy" definitions increasingly focused on trade and commercial business, until, in the eighteenth century, "men of business" in the sense of professional, commercial agents for others emerged explosively in usage, such as De Foe's in 1727: "Men of business are companions for men of business." Indeed.

Weber, mystified on this point, wrote a just-so story of his own in *The Protestant Ethic and the Spirit of Capitalism*, about a "traditional" putter-out of thread for weaving confronted by a competitor, a "modern" man of business willing to build factories. As Veblen saw clearly, the industrial revolution was actually preceded and accompanied by a financial revolution, the captains of industry swamped by competitors financed by large scale investment institutions who enabled retooling and innovation with capital infusions secured by financial instruments funded on

finance markets, all at the mere cost of everything —
ownership of enterprise. The captain of industry
transformed into a new figure not present in Marx's
physiognomy of smirking capital and cringing labor:
the manager. (What was Rickey's title, again? General
Manager. All that innovating was on behalf of owners,
who in gratitude forced him out three times, once in
St. Louis, once in Brooklyn, once in Pittsburgh.) The
growth of management is interesting.

* * *

Veblen, a quintessentially American radical,
was not aware of the colonial origins of the newer
form of capitalism he called the New Order. But what
is really colonial about that corporate structure?
Perhaps everything, at a certain level of abstraction,
but perhaps nothing, really, any more, especially as
corporate power developed in the Americas, under the
aegis of the Monroe Doctrine and its strange political
vacuum. Stories of American revolution in management sanitize the rise of financial markets and gargan-
tuan firms in the West. The joint stock company form
and the capital it made available spread throughout
the commercial world, rendering industries into businesses, especially where and when large infusions of
capital enabled reconfiguration of product and market.
The visible hand of the original, colonial joint stock
companies had often exercised sovereign power in the
colonies. This was key to the business plans of such
disparate entities as the Dutch East India Company,
the Polynesia Company, the British South Africa
Company, and the Hudson Bay Company. But partici-

pation in sovereignty was no longer central or even viable for business at home in Europe, a key moment coming when the companies themselves lost their open connection via charters to European crowns and came under the regulation of parliamentary governments. By the time the US prefers an open door policy to China, over the expensive prospect of attempting actual rule over others, be it China or Mexico or any other point south, the capacity of corporations to operate without formal participation in sovereignty is expected. Corporations, collectively, trade participation in sovereign power and direct regulation of contracts and markets for the highly useful principle of limited liability, a different kind of risk mitigation. In their operations, they became clients of a different kind of power projection, and market makers and managers of a different kind. The balance of real power between governments and companies varies enormously from place to place, but everywhere, limited liability is highly useful.

The overwhelming tendency of critical scholarship is to insist on American imperialism. But I doubt we will understand the forms of domination characteristic of American power in the twentieth century by flattening out and extending our conceptions of colony and empire, until imperialism simply means dominance, the way commodity now means thing for sale. Woodrow Wilson (the Branch Rickey of Versailles) articulated an American vision of power projection when he asked Congress on April 2, 1917, to enter World War I because "The world must be made safe for democracy." Veblen was one of the first to play off of Wilson's important phrase. In 1923, in *Absentee Ownership*, Veblen argued that America was actually "making the world safe for Big Business." Wilson's key phrase already embedded a hidden hand of its own, a hidden political hand determined and able to do the making — the global military reach of the Mahan plan is presumed and implied. From the earliest days of the Monroe Doctrine and the rise of the free states disparaged as "Banana Republics," the United States has not hesitated to use its military reach to overturn governments elsewhere. The US leads the world in this use of military force, especially in the twentieth century (see Stephen Kinser's *Overthrow*). But as Wilson had insisted in 1917,

> We desire no conquest, no dominion. We seek no indemnities for ourselves, no material compensation for the sacrifices we shall freely make. We are but one of the champions of the rights of mankind.

Veblen connected the dots with his razor-sharp ironies. In Wilson's vision, Veblen observed, "it is the soul of the country town that goes marching on," but "Meantime democracy, at least in America, has moved forward and upward to a higher business level, where larger vested interests dominate and bulkier margins of net gain are in the hazard."

Baseball, in 1945, had to measure and respond to the new world order being constituted out of US victory in the Second World War. As scholars have detailed (see John Ikenberry's *After Victory*), the United States led the world to constitute an international economic order of unprecedented complexity, a machinery of economic globalization, infrastructure for the rise of the UN, the end of the empires, and the era of decolonization. The excolony "new nations" of the UN world needed to accommodate a consortium of new, globally regulative economic institutions, a World Bank, an International (later "World") Trade Organization, an International Monetary Fund, a General Agreement on Tariffs and Trade. As European imperial preferences and trade barriers dropped, a new multilateral trading world was expected to develop. Around the detours of the Cold War, by some measures it has. But how about measures of baseball? How did baseball respond to the "separate but equal" logic that the new scheme of nation-states imposed globally, "self-determination" for the world's newly free peoples and "limited liability" of big businesses they would now entertain?

* * *

When Happy Chandler, baseball's second commissioner, was elected to the Hall of Fame in 1982, yet another Jackie Robinson debate broke out. Chandler supporters gave Chandler credit for the end of baseball's racism. His detractors scoffed. Was the end of baseball's racial barrier its moment of decolonization, its statement about the new world order of Pax Americana?

In 1946 a Steering Committee of team owners sent Happy Chandler strong advice about race and other problems facing Organized Baseball. (Their report is available in the Happy Chandler file in the library of the National Baseball Hall of Fame,

Cooperstown.) Led by Ford Frick, this committee insisted that professional baseball "is Big Business," in crisis, "its right to survive as it has always existed" threatened. Never, the Committee insisted, "has there been greater need for intelligent management and procedures to determine the common ends" and "to maintain coordination and cooperation between the various components of the baseball structure." Racists circled the wagons. But note also the renewable licensing rhetoric of management revolution, the call to bring reason to bear on traditions. "The business of Baseball has been run in the most haphazard way imaginable... we have just 'let it go.' Today, however, Baseball faces the most critical period in all its history." The committee mixed Darwinian survival with a clarion call for rights, not just survival but the right to something that has "always existed," the hyperbole of a threatened vested interest.

Let's pause here, on the meaning of "vested interest." A tragedy of Ronald Reagan's presidency is that he drove "vested interest" rhetoric out of US politics, replacing it with the remarkably different "special interests." We are drawing here and through-out, not from Veblen's first, satiric book on "conspic-uous consumption" and the leisure class, but from his later works on New Order capitalism.

Capital, to Veblen, is no longer what Smith thought it was, or what Marx thought it was. Before the advent of what Veblen called the New Order, before finance colonized industry, there was an econ-omy of markets constituted by buyers and sellers, with prices set more or less by underlying values that in turn more or less reflected labor commanded or labor congealed. Veblen is amused by Smith, spokesman for what Veblen ironically calls "the modern point of view." Veblen is respectful but ultimately more critical of Marx, who failed to notice the emerging "price system" which set prices by more profound control over the whole architecture of markets and traffic in goods. "Neither of these men," Veblen once wrote of Marx and Marx's contemporary Charles Babbage,

> is unduly bound by the traditions of economic science, and yet neither one of them was provoked by the run of the facts as he saw them to conceive the industrial system at large as a going concern. They were still content to speak of industry as an affair of detachable factors and independent segments of work going on in severalty (*Absentee Ownership*).

In fact capital and capitalism changed in the era dominated by finance markets. Veblen explained in *The Vested Interest and the Common Man*:

> Capital — at least under the new order of business enterprise — is capitalized prospective gain. From this arises one of the singularities of the current situation in business and its control of industry; viz., that the total face value, or even the total market value of the vendible securities which cover any given block of industrial equipment and material resources, and which give title to its ownership, always and greatly exceeds the total market value of the equipment and resources to

which the securities give title of ownership, and to which alone in the last resort they do give title. The margin by which the capitalized value of the going concern exceeds the value of its material properties is commonly quite wide. Only in the case of small feeble corporations, or such concerns as are balancing along the edge of bankruptcy, does this margin of intangible values narrow down and tend to disappear. Any industrial business concern which does not enjoy a margin of capitalized free earning-capacity has fallen short of ordinary business success and is possessed of no vested interest.

This margin of free income which is capitalized in the value of the going concern comes out of the net product of industry over cost. It is secured by successful bargaining and an advantageous position in the market... In case the free income which is gained in this way promises to continue, it presently becomes a vested right. It may then be formally capitalized as an immaterial asset having a recognized earning-capacity equal to this prospective free income. That is to say, the outcome is a capitalized claim to get something for nothing; which constitutes a vested interest.

In the New Order, the valuation of capital itself, starting with shares of stock in companies, abandoned the Lockean semiotic of looking in nature for the value-referent, an idea embedded in the original idea of selling shares in the companies "stock," i.e. property of various kinds. The new order is the realization, dream or nightmare, of a self-consciously pragmatic semiosis, trading on values realizable only in future transactions, thus immaterial as Veblen insists.

Organized Baseball was exactly this kind of vested interest, and Ford Frick's steering committee knew it. Frick's committee was out above all to school the new commissioner and the other owners on the need to sustain a common plan to address key business issues, such as race. The committee recommended above all a permanent Executive Council to advise the commissioner — something like themselves. They recommended strengthening the reserve clause, "the fundamental upon which the entire structure of Professional Baseball is based," against legal challenges, player raids (especially "the Mexican raids"), and union organizing. Then came the "race question."

Frick's committee knew that Americans cared more about excellence than "color, race or creed," and cited the fame of "great Negro athletes" and even the heroism of their war service. It felt history impinging. Black athletes had been football All-Americans, Olympic heroes (in Berlin), boxing champions. But:

> Professional Baseball is a private business enterprise. It has to depend on profits for its existence, just like any other business. It is a business in which Negroes, as well as Whites, have substantial investments in parks, franchises, and players contracts. Professional baseball, both Negro and White, has grown and prospered over a period of many years on the basis of separate leagues. The employment of a Negro on one AAA League club [Jackie Robinson then played for Dodgers' farm club Montreal in the International League] in 1946 resulted in a tremendous increase in Negro attendance at all games in which the player appeared.

The percentage of Negro attendance at some games at Newark and Baltimore was in excess of 50%. A situation might be presented, if Negroes participate in Major League games, in which the preponderance of Negro attendance in parks such as Yankee Stadium, the Polo Grounds and Comiskey Park could conceivably threaten the value of the Major League franchises owned by these Clubs.

The report then doubted, myopically, that many black players were ready for the Major Leagues. With baseball integration the Negro Leagues, a two-million dollar annual business, "will eventually fold up — the investments of their club owners will be wiped out — and a lot of professional Negro players will lose their jobs." (This was true.) And finally, their businesses were intertwined, especially where Negro League teams rented stadiums from Organized Baseball. "Club owners in the major leagues are reluctant to give up revenues amounting to hundreds of thousands of dollars every year."

Ironically, given the later importance of the lonely man, the Frick committee sought to shift the problem back to leagues: "the relationship of the Negro player, and/or the existing Negro Leagues to professional Baseball is a real problem — one that affects all Baseball." Frick's committee urged "all Baseball" to leave this problem to the new Executive Council. No single Club should do anything that "could conceivably result in lessening the value of several Major League franchises." They were well aware that the "individual action of any one Club may exert tremendous pressures upon the whole structure" and called for considered solution to the "overall problem" instead.

Beyond the Shadow of the Senators, Brad Snyder's excellent history of the Grays games in Washington, documents the failed hopes there, and the role of rental income in Clark Griffith's opposition to integration. Griffith pondered a new playoff structure to Major League baseball, a series after the World Series between the Major League champions and the Negro League champions. Lucrative barnstorming tours pitted white teams versus black ones (John Holway documents that black teams won more often, in Autumn games played largely in the South). Some Lords of the Game were even willing to reconsider the pinnacle structure rather than disturb purity they felt intrinsic to the value of their franchises.

Happy Chandler never got along well with the owners. Despite a 15-1 owners' vote against integrating baseball at the 1946 annual meeting, he allowed Rickey to promote his black player to the Major Leagues without invoking "the best interests of baseball" against it. By the late 1950s Organized Baseball was massively transformed, not only integrated by race (the Yankees were second to last; the Red Sox were last), but also better integrated nationally, with two teams on the west coast, and the Braves in Atlanta. So, Chandler brought Organized Baseball into the new world order by promoting inclusion, erasing barriers?

* * *

The buttoned-down, franchise-value focus of Ford Frick's committee report has not stopped historians from correctly labeling it a last ditch effort to defend Jim Crow. Was Frick outside Organized Baseball's mainstream? Hardly: after seventeen years as President of the National League, he succeeded Chandler as the third Commissioner of Baseball, and was enshrined in the Hall of Fame in 1970, more than a decade before the Veterans Committee elected Chandler. Chandler was right to overrule in favor of the anti-racism sweeping the world's institutions in the New World Order, a world of formal symmetries in rights and formal, legal equality. But to understand how Chandler also defended the vested interests of his Big Business, and renovated its specific and (nationally, racially, but not internationally) capacious purity in a world of emerging nation-states, we can introduce the Mexican League controversy via Happy Chandler's own memoirs.

Chandler, like most baseball historians, treats the episode as humorous. The threat to baseball was serious, he asserts, but his tone suggests something else. The "rich and colorful Jorge Pasquel" was "handsome, canny, articulate, and eccentric." Other sources describe an immaculate, cosmopolitan dresser. Chandler remembers a "silver encrusted gaucho gunbelt with two gleaming pistols." Pasquel, effective in signing several Major League all-stars, is the butt of jokes in Chandler's account of his conversations with players, notably Stan Musial and Ted Williams ("He was laughing up his sleeve"), versus "poor Mickey" Owen, who made a "big mistake." Vern Stephens, AL home run leader in 1945, jumped back after only two games. "I learned later why he came back — their diet of beans and tortillas and their casual lifestyle was too much for him." Chandler's narrative is too extreme to be entirely coherent:

> They were playing crazy baseball in Mexico. Not the same kind of rules we use. The Pasquels just made a show out of the game.... Their idea of 'beisbol' was simply stupid.
>
> These raids were serious.

Chandler's main complaint was not that the Mexicans wanted a new World Series. That was beyond his imagination. He responded to a threat to the reserve clause, a change in players' contract options and value. If players could "jump" to the Mexican League after years of development, then even farm systems couldn't make the world safe for Major League rosters (whereas Rickey, in his Cardinals glory days, did not buy a player from another organization for his Major League roster for over a decade). Investment in farm systems would not keep labor cheap and its flow secure; nightmarishly, the extensive costs of the farm system would continue without control of players and salaries it was designed to insure. The Pasquel brothers, investors invigorating the syndicated Mexican League, offered Chandler a generous supplemental salary of $50,000, equal to his salary with Organized Baseball, if he would become the Commissioner of the Mexican League also. Chandler wrote in his memoirs: "The Pasquel brothers were totally outlaw operators, and were not at all interested in what was decent and beneficial for the major leagues in the United States."

Jorge Pasquel and his brothers were very serious about transforming the Mexican League into a major league rival to the National League and the American League. Married to the daughter of one Mexican President, and friends with his two successors, Pasquel was well positioned to try. His eight team league signed twenty-seven of the 1945 US Major League players, usually for salaries many times higher than previous, and made offers to many more. Aware of the talent coming home from war, Pasquel thought his timing was perfect. He knew his circuit would need larger and better ballparks to be profitable, and probably a redistribution of franchise locations. Enabled by his syndicate structure, he experimented, changing player assignments. He did not expect the open and extensive sabotage he soon faced.

Invoking the "best interests of baseball" clause, Happy Chandler banned the players who "jumped" to the Mexican League from returning to Organized Baseball for five years. This was the centerpiece of Organized Baseball's response, and it was effective. One-time Mexican League players who did not stay, such as Max Lanier and Danny Gardella, were eventually reduced to playing for semi-pro teams in the US, and in the wake of Jackie Robinson even teams in the Negro Leagues were reluctant to play them for fear of jeopardizing their players' status in Organized Baseball. Chandler didn't just ban the players, but banned all professionals who played with or against the "outlaw" players, from contracts with Organized Baseball.

That was why Chandler was in Havana in 1947, explaining that only the US game was "clean": he sought to extend the ban against "jumpers" and their Mexican League associates. (That Spring, Lanier pitched brilliantly on very short rest to lead one of the oldest professional baseball teams in the world, Almendares, to victory in the Cuban League.) The Cubans resisted, initially. When the established Cuban League acceded to pressure and agreed to respect the reserve clause and reject banned players, Cuban baseball split into two leagues. The established Cuban League gained players from Organized Baseball. The new league, the Liga de la Federación (the Federation League) built rosters around Cubans who were Mexican League stars. But it did not pose a sustained threat to the Cuban League, which had established fan followings and the deep new source of talent, above all because the heat around the Mexican League dissipated. Many talented players were allowed and encouraged to "jump" back to the Cuban League at the end of the Liga de la Federación season in 1948, just in time for the Cuban League's playoffs. The Liga de la Federación folded after one full year of play (see González Echevarría's *The Pride of Havana* for an extensive account).

Banning and blacklisting caused the Pasquels' effort to fail, and they abandoned it after a year. But it wasn't the only sabotage they faced. Louisville Slugger would not sell them the same bats they sold to Organized Baseball. Nor could they obtain the same balls. The Pasquels did some sabotaging of their own when players attempted to leave Mexico, enlisting state aid to block their exit. Having white American players tailed to insure that they stayed put alienated many of them. But perhaps the most outrageous sabotaging of the Mexican League came not from Organized Baseball, but from a more desperate, longer-standing rival. To really understand everything happening here, as baseball in Mexico, Cuba, and elsewhere in Latin America underwent a profound upheaval, we have to look beyond the merely dyadic dynamic between the Mexican League and Organized Baseball. More was going on.

Organized Baseball responded swiftly and fiercely to a threat that came from a rival that they misunderstood as clownish. The Mexican League also had longer term enemies: the owners of Negro League teams. For the Negro Leagues, the Mexican League was not a new rival. Contract jumping was an old and expensive problem for investors in Negro League baseball (see Lanctot's excellent history). Negro League players frequently jumped to Caribbean and especially Mexican League teams. For their attempted breakout 1946 season, the Pasquels' twenty-seven Major Leaguers were joined by at least twenty-five Negro League veterans, ten of whom were mid-season Mexican League all-stars. In fact, the Pasquels became irritated with their expensive white stars, and the players were restive on salary issues, because as Jorge Pasquel put it (quoted in Pietrusza), the white players were being "thoroughly outclassed by tan performers."

Black players came to the Mexican League for higher salaries, but also for better working conditions. US Hall of Famer Willie Wells began play in Mexico in 1940 after seventeen years with the St. Louis Stars, the Homestead Grays, the Kansas City Monarchs, the Newark Eagles and other Negro League teams. He was impressed. "We are heroes here," he said. "In the United States everything I did was regulated by color. Well, here in Mexico I am a man." The Negro Leagues team owners could not compete with the Pasquels financially. So, as James Overmyer has shown, team owners Etta Manley and Cum Posey (both recently elected to the Hall of Fame) attempted during the world war to change the draft status of players intending to "jump" to Mexico, notifying draft boards that they were leaving their defense-related jobs.

Observers within Organized Baseball were overwhelmingly skeptical of the Mexican League's chances to establish itself as a Major League in 1946, a skepticism still sustained in most baseball history books to date. The core of the skepticism was that, once the Major Leagues in the US adjusted to a new pay scale, and the Mexicans took their salary offers to a level sustainable by their likely long run income, there was just no way the Mexican League would be able to convince real Major League talent to play there. Why would Major Leaguers endure heat without air-conditioning, lesser ballparks, and an alien language and culture?

But as Roberto González Echevarría has forcefully argued, this analysis misses the main point. Alien language and culture to whom? Of the first eight Major Leaguers signed by Jorge Pasquel in winter 1946, only Danny Gardella was a US citizen. The other seven all spoke Spanish already. Further, the

Mexican League was the common destination for black Latin American players, even from Cuba, who faced more discrimination in Cuba than they did in Mexico. The black US players were following a path shown them by black Cuban teammates in the Negro Leagues. As González Echevarría summarizes,

> Mexico's allure to non-American players is a factor not generally considered when assessing the reaction of organized baseball to Pasquel's "raids." The majority of these, like Agapito Mayor, Sandalio Consuegra, and Andres Fleitas, were Cuban. But there were also Puerto Ricans and Venezuelans. Not to mention, of course, that any Mexican talent being developed would most likely remain at home. At the beginning of the 1946-47 Cuban League season the best Latin American players were affiliated with Mexican teams and went to Havana for the winter. Most were making more money that way than many players in the majors and far more than they could hope to earn in the minors. Organized baseball was not only in danger of losing its own stars, but also the increasingly abundant Latin pool, particularly rich now that Latin blacks (such as Orestes Minoso) would be allowed to sign with major-league teams.

Sabotage of potential rivals' opportunities to produce a competing version of a complex commodity was, Veblen thought, the most flamboyant, common, and significant tactic of vested interests out to continue to dominate terms of trade and thereby to sustain their receipt of something for nothing. Whether or not they fully gleaned the threat to their pinnacle status as baseball's dominant powers, the Major Leagues knew that the Mexican League involved lots that they did not like. While the rules for decolonization and ex-colony nation-state formation were being hammered out, and just before the growing shadow of the Cold War would change and polarize the terms of order, Organized Baseball led by Chandler, Griffith, and others did more than just sabotage the Mexican League. With the grinding collapse of the Negro Leagues, also, opportunity for black Latin players was an open issue. And for everyone who played baseball, "winter ball" was a useful player development tool. Chandler acted to insure open doors for the Major League clubs, and limited aspirations for everyone else. He made the world safe, for his big business.

The first piece was the arrangement already described, with the Cuban League. On June 10, 1947, the Cuban League, a winter league, joined the National Association of Professional Baseball Leagues, the organization that regulated minor league baseball within Organized Baseball's "National Agreement." Less than two months into Jackie Robinson's Major League career, the reserve clause was reaching its way into the Caribbean via mutual recognition of the leagues and their contracts. Within a year, Organized Baseball had similar working agreements with winter leagues in Puerto Rico, Panama, and Venezuela. Each nation-state got a league of their own. Chandler officially lifted all the bans and suspensions when Danny Gardella began to get traction in court, and the Lords of the Game felt pressure, again, on the reserve clause. That same year, 1949, the Caribbean winter leagues affiliated with Organized Baseball arranged the first "Caribbean Series."

Thus Latin American baseball came into a format more to the liking of the US Major Leagues: one league per country and vice versa, and a two-way street for development of prospects that was actually built to be a ladder leading up to the US pinnacle leagues. The Cubans, their professional league again unified, won seven of the first twelve Caribbean Series, befitting the strength of Cuban baseball. Then something happened in Cuba, Castro's revolution, and the Cold War overwrote this baseball architecture. The Caribbean Series was cancelled in 1961, and not revived until 1970. Cuba, its ties with Organized Baseball long in abeyance, was left out, as was Panama. The two new invitees were the Dominican Republic, an emerging baseball powerhouse, and Mexico, which had finally signed its own minor league deal with Organized Baseball in 1955.

Game Theory

Baseball may have been born in America, but now it belongs to the world.

—Bud Selig

The American game is looking less and less American every year.... For the first time, a chance to reclaim the game for America.

—Karl Ravech on ESPN's *Sportscenter*

Our game is too international as it is.

—Mark McGwire

If we allow Japan a separate deal, it would ruin the whole business model.

—Jim Small, managing director of MLB Japan

They were not prepared for the greatness of the event.

—Jesus Alou, former MLB player

Unlike other baseball books, this one is also intended to contribute to anthropological theory and the cultural study of American power. My historical realism descends from substantivism in the history of economic anthropology. Substantivism is the school in economic anthropology that locates economic systems within cultural orders, skeptical of formal, universal modes of description of economic means, ends, and motives. The substantivists debated with the formalists, and in the 1980s their debate was subsumed in the rise of historical anthropology, with and without Marxist premises. Gradually, over time, assertions of a political economic substructure to real history returned culture to an epiphenomenal status for many theorists, especially those following Eric Wolf's call, in the preface to *Europe and the People Without History*, for a new, historically oriented political economy. My own commitment is instead to the structural, historical anthropology proposed by Marshall Sahlins, with French and Boasian roots, which locates sometimes rapid economic change within histories of cultural structure. I have already explained my reservations about elementary forms, and predilection for the study of culturally informed constitution and reconception of real objects, my Weberian revision of Latour. New things like baseball and Organized Baseball and the WBC in particular, games and joint stock companies in general, change the conditions of possibility for action. Thus the historical realist problematic is tracking reason and practical culture, the history of reason in its relations to changing real possibilities.

In the late twentieth century, theory changed significantly in Economics as well as in Anthropology, but in a radically different direction. While Anthropology turned to history, Economics turned from scarcity-based allocation models to risk-based game models, from scarcity to games. Economics was taken over from within, especially in the US, by a mathematically powerful new paradigm. Game theory, in Economics, Political Science and elsewhere, is blind to cultural difference and deliberately reductionistic toward historical specificity, and unconscious of its own cultural dimensions especially when its practitioners actually build and add games to the real. We now need a substantivist anthropology to analyze the actual cultural history of risk, of games, and of the consequences of the development and use of tools for the analysis, manipulation, and construction of both. The deployment of game analytics, the building of an economy of games, has been a major consequence of US political, social and intellectual dominance, and it requires much closer, historically realist, cultural, and institutional analysis than it has received.

* * *

Game theory proper enters Economics after World War II, but actually begins in military theory, as Philip Mirowski's *Machine Dreams* details. Its chronotopics, to use another Bakhtinian concept — in other words, the spacetime landscape it supposes and projects as the framework of analytic possibilities — is remarkably different from scarcity-based economic theory. The realism of scarcity-based economics was always a moral theory, really more in the tradition of Malthus than Smith. It was the duty of the trained Economist to determine the maximal possibilities of limited situations, an anti-utopian prospect suitable to a sober, responsible, disinterested character, ready to accept what the world has in store. Game theory drags the economic puritan from the church of limits into a battle-filled casino. The realism of game-based Economics is still a moral realism, not an historical realism, and is still reductionistic, seeking universal features to all situations, just different features: now there are always opposing wills or forces, risks and stakes, opportunity costs making resource allocation a mere special case. The scarcity and game approaches also share some features: along with reductionism and universal modeling, they share the premise of incipience, a much favored moral doctrine in the US, the idea that starting fresh is better, that nothing that has come before really should matter. In Economics, especially following Coase and Becker, a new dream also opens, an economics of everything, a new institutional economics that is not just a theory of the economy (the project Weber found doomed, because of economically relevant non-economic causes), and not the older institutional economics which, following the likes of Weber and Veblen, insisted on the irreducibility of institutions in the orientation of economic action. The new institutional economics, on the paradigm of Coase's theory of the firm, opened the prospect that economic theory might explain the nature of all important institutions. Along with this new form of universal came a pragmatist turn in the epistemology of models: if scarcity theory had aspired to describe an existing, actual universe, game theory is more than content with heuristic standing for its simplifications, since its purpose is to generate new and better outcomes, to understand the world by changing it.

While economists and many political scientists found more and more within a world of games, US policy makers and corporate managers increasingly relied on economists and other game theorists for models, and deployed the new economics of risk assessment in myriad ways. Games ruthlessly detach their elements from context, clear a field, substitute purified issues and outcomes for real complexity, dramatize process, heroize and demonize parties in conflict, and teach pursuit of victory. Warfare, investment, democracy and "nation-building," even global health policy all become the subjects of game analysis that, incipiently, becomes its own basis for organizing intervention and action. The way ordinary things can become commodities for sale, they become games. Opponents and other "players" are taught the rules, implicitly and often explicitly.

Meanwhile, Organized Baseball invents its own new genre of championship, potentially disturbing its World Series, its pinnacle event for a century. What drives them to change the structure of their game? My point is not that it is a project in game theory, but rather that we could use some insight into a larger cultural history of actual game building. What was built in to the design and accomplished by the launching of this World Baseball Classic, Inc.? Can an irreductive historical realism encompass the wisdom of dehistoricizing theory by rehistoricizing the building of actual games? The first step to an irreductive approach to their new project is to look for the actual ends the organizers pursue.

* * *

Therefore, here are a few somewhat more concrete problems: (1) why didn't Organized Baseball continue simply to sabotage all international championship tournaments? After years of resisting Olympic tournaments and Baseball World Cups, why suddenly invent your own?; (2) why stage a world championship during Spring Training? Why not the proper time for a pinnacle championship, the end of the season?; (3) Why did the World Baseball Classic play "trailblazer" films between innings on the electronic scoreboards at every venue? Why single out players from each nation who succeeded in Major League Baseball, and develop all possible comparison to Jackie Robinson? In connection to this, why has Major League Baseball become Robinson-obsessed? Selig loves the rules, with a single exception:

> Throughout its long history, Major League Baseball has operated under the premise that no single person is bigger than the game — no single person other than Jackie Robinson (quoted by AP

while retiring Robinson's number throughout
Organized Baseball, on April 17, 1997).

Why does Organized Baseball so love Jackie
Robinson?

At greater abstraction, (4) Why are nations
suddenly so important in baseball, allegedly undergoing
globalization? Why are national emblems so warmly
embraced by the fans at the World Baseball Classic?
How does nationalism change the game, and vice
versa? (5) What does imposition of a new game do to
existing political conflicts? Creating new places for
flags and national rivalries, can baseball avoid existing
conflicts? Is it commenting on them? The Olympic
movement has a clear political message. Does baseball?
Is a baseball movement emergent, any comment on
East and West or North and South by way of the
games? Can baseball avoid world politics the way it so
long avoided world competition? And, the ultimate, (6)
What does Organized Baseball want out of this? What
are its strategies and tactics? Are they working?

* * *

Timing is everything, for both of the first two
questions. Why the world tourney now, and why in
Spring?

The planners of the World Baseball Classic
offer abundant explanations to both. Russell Gabay,
San Juan venue manager for Major League Baseball,
talked with Ben Eastman and me on the off day
between rounds in San Juan. Gabay said that the goals
of the Classic, beyond the obvious purpose of making

money, were to bring the world's best players together, and to develop baseball as a world game. Without Olympic baseball, he argued, development funding for baseball will erode all over the world, unless new inspiration arises. Gene Orza, head of the Players' Union, discussed timing with sportswriters on the field in San Diego before the final. Orza claimed that logistical factors dominated the scheduling. Fewer players would have agreed to play a November tournament, with more training camp and games after the long season. March scheduling was difficult, especially getting players back to regular training camps before the end of spring training. He was pleased that conversation was about how to improve the schedule — perhaps finals in the All-star break in July — and not whether to hold the tournament again. In any case, another March schedule for all or most of the tournament was inevitable for 2009. And if the Japanese won, they will argue that they are entitled to host next time. It will be discussed.

Like all comments from management to journalists — our clear role in both conversations — these are not just partial truths but deliberately self-promoting partial truths. Ethnographers are always in the business of partial truths, but what a Gene Orza provides is professional partial truth, even major league. So we need other angles of view. Strikingly, Orza's perspective was dominated by demands of the Major League schedule and contracts. Were there no other considerations? A comparison on timing tactics will help.

* * *

Bud Selig has promoted April 15th as a permanent memorial day. He probably wouldn't mind if it became a national or global holiday, also. But at least in Organized Baseball, April 15th, Jackie Robinson Day, is almost as much a command performance as retiring Robinson's number. (Baseball insiders have a pious strategic explanation for retiring the number: children at ballparks major and minor, across the land, will ask, "And why is number 42 retired?") But let us ask, why April 15th? That's the day Robinson entered the Dodgers lineup. But why then? If you know baseball, you can see that it's a strange time to add a rookie to the line-up. April 15th is just after the regular season has begun. If it was time, why didn't he start the season in the Majors? Or was he being forced in? Not in a strategic sense, but a tactical one, what was Rickey doing?

To be clear, tactics like tactile is about touching. Strategy is planning. Tactical decisions come when already in contact, especially with an opponent. Game theory is all about counteracting anticipated moves of opponents (rather than merely optimizing allocations of scarce goods). But the unforeseen, also, can force changes in tactics, including what Weber called "unintended consequences of intentional actions" (Jason Giambi once hit a home run while trying to foul a pitch off) and also entirely unconnected things, people and situations that impinge radically on the relevant elements. Robinson entered the Majors on April 15th when Rickey reacted tactically to an unforeseen development.

Arthur Mann, in his 1951 book *Baseball Confidential*, describes events as a Dodger insider. All Spring, 1947, Rickey was planning Robinson's entry to the Majors. We can recall that Frick had already led the other clubs to vote 15-1 against allowing Rickey to proceed. Rickey wanted resistance to black players to face a counter-force, the team's obvious needs and the player's skills. He feared accusation that he was acting by "force or fiat." In fact he feared that integration like prohibition could be set back decades if it was imposed too aggressively. As Mann put it, "he counted solely on Robinson's skill at hitting or handling a baseball to decide the issue on the ball field and nowhere else." Above all, Rickey wanted the Dodger players to regard the move as necessary from "their pardonably selfish interests, i.e., winning ball games and a pennant."

In Spring Training 1947 Robinson hit .625 in minor league camp while five candidates failed, Mann claims, trying out for the Dodgers' first base job. Leo Durocher, the Dodgers' manager, favored bringing Robinson onto the Dodgers, and some baseball writers wanted an end to the "phony suspense." But Rickey was worried more when "sidetracked by the unexpected... a letter from Dixie Walker, asking to be traded." Walker, a star, was traded. Then, April 9th, while Rickey heard from Durocher that he and the coaches were ready for Robinson, and some of the players had come around, they all received stunning news: Durocher was suspended for a year. Happy Chandler had determined that Durocher's consorting with gamblers was a threat to the best interests of baseball.

We can leave aside whose act of sabotage this was: Mann's book, subtitled *Secret History of the War among Chandler, Durocher, MacPhail, and Rickey*, was written to blame the Yankees' Lee MacPhail. Rickey had to respond to disaster. When Walker had to go, competitive goals were harmed. But Durocher was both the barometer of potential clubhouse resistance, and the rock against which it was to break uselessly. (Earlier that Spring, when told that Dixie Walker and others were preparing a petition against Robinson joining the Dodgers, Durocher told them they could wipe a particular body part with it.) There was no use waiting anymore for Durocher to consolidate the situation in the clubhouse, and too much risk letting new dynamics develop there. Further, another tactical consideration, Rickey wanted whatever limits he could get on press coverage of Robinson's controversial first day. (Dodgers broadcasters did not mention Robinson's race all year.) Early on April 10th, 1947, Robinson signed a Major League contract. Newspapers debating the Durocher suspension were given notice of Robinson's promotion, "a whisper in a whirlwind." Most accounts of Jackie Robinson breaking the color line do not dwell on the impact of Durocher's suspension. But these whispers in the whirlwind are worth understanding: they separate real games from games in theory.

* * *

Strategy, and tactics, then: why did the world need a nationalist baseball event, in the era of globalization? And who wanted it?

No doubt the players wanted it, Rickey's audience of final measure. The players' enthusiasm for the World Baseball Classic was a theme in advertising for it, so again we deal with major leaguers in the game of partial truth. But they showed up, and none held out for payment. Second, Cuba wanted it. The roiled waters of Cuban-US relations almost destroyed the tournament, when the US Treasury Department cited trade boycott policy and denied the Cuban team its visas. Conservative Cuban exile voices (and Yale's González Echevarría) applauded this decision, pushed for US embargo of Cuban slave labor and all things Castro-connected, and suggested that an expatriate Cuban team could play instead of a team actually from Cuba. Third, in an extraordinary show of unanimity, the world of amateur baseball wanted it, especially the Caribbean powers therein. Via the International Baseball Federation, who were sanctioning the tourney, Caribbean baseball leaders insisted on a tournament with the Cubans, meaning the team from Cuba. Puerto Rican baseball officials refused to host if Cubans were denied visas, and Venezuela offered to host the rounds in which Cuba played, obviating the need for US visas. Instead, financial details were rearranged with the Cubans donating all profits, and the Bush administration backed down, saving the site architecture the WBC had arranged.

But who wanted the WBC to be so nationalistic?

This is a more profound question than it might appear, as memory can clarify. In the 1930s and

1940s audiences liked baseball games based on racial opposition, games between black teams and white teams. Which race played baseball better, was thought an interesting and entertaining question. The breaking of baseball's color barrier was part of a global sea change in race practices, change in public morality, and etiquette in racial identification. It is no longer acceptable to stage a game between teams based upon race. Why then are games between nations such a good idea?

The nation-state idea has gone through many phases as it has moved from Wilsonian utopia to third world nightmare. According to Peter Balakian in *The Burning Tigris*, the inspiration for Wilson's global political strategy came two decades before Wilson articulated his 14 points and led Versailles diplomats to begin the manufacture of nation-states out of empires. Wilson first saw national "self-determination" as the moral alternative to imperial domination when contemplating the Armenian genocide. If only this Christian nation, trapped in an Islamic empire, could be free. Since Versailles, American liberal theory has insisted (and since World War II presumed) that democracy is best realized in the nation-state format. Nations are now defined not as races or peoples but by their possession of a state, and states are legitimate only if they express political will of a nation. The strange new idea of nation-building was born, the other side of the coin of state-building in the decolonizing world. It is a game played by given rules, above all that no other forms of political will and action were legitimate, especially wars of conquest. In

outcome, the poor, the small, and the marginal gain the
freedom of self-determination, the telos of independence, but their democratic rights extinguish utterly at
the border. They have no right of influence anywhere
else. They certainly do not gain control over the
planet's other leviathans, the big corporations.

In a world of substantively uneven powers,
leverage and life chances connected to different flags
and other vested interests, when and why would
anyone embrace the flag of a minor or even middle-
rank power on the world stage?

Middle class fans filled baseball stadiums for
the World Baseball Classic, wearing national colors and
waving national flags. Their fervor and their taste for
official gear surprised the marketers. The official
Puerto Rico team hats sold out at the first Puerto Rico
game in San Juan in Round Two, even though the official hats cost $22 and up, and $5 Puerto Rico baseball
hats were ubiquitously available from hawkers outside
the ballpark. Fans wanted to wear World Baseball
Classic stuff at World Baseball Classic games. In San
Juan, the day of the first Puerto Rico-Cuba game,
2,500 official hats were sold, to a crowd totaling
slightly less than 20,000 (plus the small crowd, mostly
series ticket holders, at the Panama-Netherlands game
earlier that day). Something like 10% of the people in
the stands that day wore an official baseball hat that
they had just bought. Generally, first round merchandise sales "exceeded the sales numbers that were
projected for the entire 17 day event," according to the
World Baseball Classic News and Notes for March 13,
2006.

Ben Eastman observed while we watched a second round game in San Juan that we won't fully understand the euphoria of the fans dressing in national team emblems — game jerseys or T-shirts, with flags or team names blazoned, hats with country flags and symbols, faces painted with flag colors or replica flags — until we can connect their particular intensity with the events on the field and their relations to those events. Without reviewing the history of crowds (for a strong and probing discussion see Stanley Tambiah's *Leveling Crowds*), sports crowds have, I think, a longing for rapture. Fans hope for the moment of unity, collected will, that dissolves mundane concerns and limits. The crowd heightens the experience of the fan, especially in the roar when a key event changes their team's fortunes, or caps them with significant victory. The commodious inner world of the ballpark has somehow gained a particular poignancy for a national imaginary hungry to affiliate with victory.

Ray Fogelson has labeled "sports totemism" this wearing of team colors, jerseys and paraphernalia to games. This totemism, and pursuit of rapture, is not new in sports crowds. It took on a particular fervor and style, though, in the nationalist crowds at the WBC. These crowds were not like the Cubs fans in the bleachers at Wrigley Field every day; ethnographer Holly Swyers has well described the Cub fans' shared experience, their subtle, ironic communication, and the rituals, routines and gestures that constitute them as a unique community with its own history. The fervor of the nationalist crowd was less face to face and more imaginary, in Benedict Anderson's sense, sharing an ideal first of all even when seated together. Second, they had a far more intense, at times tangible, present fervor, more entirely devoted to the prospect of winning.

Part of the enthusiasm, in San Juan, was the spectacle of significant, pinnacle games played in the Caribbean itself. The emotion was palpable as Puerto Ricans saw heroes finally get to play crucial games at home, and past success seemed to elevate Bernie Williams above all others. When Williams hit a home run that set up victory for Puerto Rico over Cuba in round one, and later when he won the most valuable player award for the round, the crowd called him out for a "curtain call." Williams, whose extensive World Series success has made him an all-time leader in many post-season and World Series categories, told reporters that "It was one of the most important hits of my career; it's like playing the World Series here." Emphasis on "here."

But if these home games were crucial to the enthusiasm, there was also a strong diasporic dimension to the crowds. Many Puerto Rico supporters returned to the island for the games, from newer homes in the US. The fans for other teams were largely diasporic, including large numbers of Cuban and Dominican permanent residents of Puerto Rico. Yet fans in the crowd embraced un-hyphenated nationality: "I am Dominican," "We are Cubans." Literature on sports is sometimes an unintentional parody of anthropological analysis, propounding on the "tribalism" of fans. Especially concerning fan violence in football/soccer, simple-minded evolutionary models inform description of hooligans as some kind of atavism. Regardless what model of and for crowd behavior motivates football's violence, violence was absent, even signs of real fear or hatred absent, at the WBC. (In San Juan, a man in a Red Sox hat lunged and caught a foul ball, and then yelled "Yankees suck! Yankees suck!" while dancing to celebrate his feat; laughter followed him as intended, exuberant and ironic.) Far from a display of ascribed or obligatory, grim and determined business, the tournament for its fans had the texture of masquerade. A main chance was at hand to pursue a fantasy. Baseball has, available in it, the commodious fantasy of rural virtues relived for the urbanite, a masquerade as Sons of Soil. For diaspora nationalism, this capacity of the game's imagery redoubles with the guilt and redemption of a failed and largely abandoned nation-state utopia. Or at least a redemption in masquerade. (Another T-shirt at the ballpark in San Juan said "Gracias Fidel Viva Puerto Rico," which Ben Eastman glossed as thanking Fidel for inspiring relocation.) While in this world of baseball, while taken out to the ball game, taken out to the crowd (to recall the famous song) these fans were there with the nation they would will to victory, beyond all complexities of where they lived and why. They had a chance, even against the leviathans. Regardless of private accommodations with power these resettled people had already made in diasporic movement, they could participate in the Levy-Bruhlian style of crowds, with the team in national victory. Thus these crowds connected passionately with their teams.

And when it was over, when Puerto Rico lost to Cuba in the game that ended Puerto Rico's run and sent Cuba on to San Diego, most Puerto Rican fans were quick to remove their overshirt Puerto Rico jerseys, to roll up their flags. Many even took off their

Figure 5. Cheering for the Puerto Rican team

hats, crowd streaming from the stadium in a collective act of removing their costumes — but not the expat Cubans who had won. Of whatever political stripe, mostly anti-Castro, they reveled in victory, chanting and posing for pictures (proving Sontag half right). We saw no threats or flares of violence between the two groups. Fan reveling is famous in Latin American international baseball, for visiting teams especially, and lasts all game long, good news and bad, but with special intensity in victory. International away games are carnivals for diasporic people.

For the World Baseball Classic, this was not limited to the Caribbean. Korean-American support for the Korean team was extraordinary. All of the hats and most of the shirts with "Korea" on them sold out early. Against Japan in the semi-finals, despite a mid-game collapse which ruined Korea's chance at the final, and in pelting rain, in a rain delay, a Korean crowd slamming thundersticks and dressed to the nines in the team's shade of blue chanted and sang in support of the team. Since most of it was in Korean, I asked our seat-mate, a Korean-American electronics entrepreneur from San Jose who owned his own business, what was being said. "We are chanting it's okay, we don't care, because we won already," he said. "We take the result but we don't accept that we lost." He told me the Korean team manager had said, "we are already the winner, but have to play again." (The Korean team defeated Japan twice, and finished with a better overall record, 6-1 versus 5-3 for Japan and also for Cuba.) The Korean crowd was disappointed, to be sure, but also insistent on continuing the fun available, celebrating victories and serenading their heroic team. It was not depressed or agonizing. Few sat like some stunned Venezuelan or Puerto Rican fans had in San Juan, unmoving as the stadium emptied after their teams lost decision games on the final play. In San Diego, the Korean(-American) crowd booed pro-Japan signs projected from stadium-cams on the scoreboard (one, with the Japanese flag, saying "revenge"), and cheered images of Korean signs and thundersticks, also an American flag. When play resumed and the Japanese hit into an out on the first pitch, they went wild. Why? "For fun." It was an escapist self-crafting, a self-sustaining rapture that did not require the final. It much resembled the longstanding dream of Red Sox nation, just to beat the Yankees for once. The chance was taken to remind the Japanese about two Korean victories. Ichiro had aggressively pronounced hopes for Japanese supremacy, and the Korean crowd was heavy, also with signs about Ichiro. But one got the distinct impression that they were happier to have his comments to play with. Korean-Japanese hatreds can run deep, but here they did not. Baseball and national-ism trade in a sublimated erotics of victory.

* * *

Limits to political expression also emerged, early, in the World Baseball Classic. On March 9th, as Cuba played The Netherlands, the crowd behind home plate crowd was stirred into a small tempest by fans holding up anti-Castro signs. Like advertisers, they targeted the captive television audience. It was said that 90 % of televisions in Cuba watched the

WBC games; the signs said "Peloteros Sí, Castro No" (Baseball Players Yes, Castro No), "Peloteros Sí, Tiranos No," (Baseball Players Yes, Tyrants No) and "Abajo Fidel" (Down with Fidel). Cuban team officials and stadium security tried to confiscate the signs, but San Juan police protected the right of citizens to freedom of speech. A police officer stood with the protesters in the late innings.

The next day, MB Sports, official WBC promoter in San Juan, posted a "code of conduct" policy on posters and announced it over loudspeakers during games. Efforts to protest continued, but stadium security was unhindered in suppressing them, confiscating posters at the gate, forcing people to cover T-shirts that spelled out political messages. The posted policy seemed written to address anxieties of a Puerto Rican national citizenship, with something to prove on the international stage. (A version was also posted in San Diego, but it is hard to say what it meant there; we saw no one reading it.) The policy concluded:

> The World Baseball Classic is an internationally recognized event that has allowed Puerto Rican fans (in San Juan this shifted to "United States fans") and their guests the opportunity of enjoying the best baseball in the world, while at the same time has allow Puerto Rico ("has allowed the United States") positive exposure in the world. We urge all fans to recognize the importance of this unique event and guarantee its success by observing these rules.

But the attitude of the San Diego fans around us — we were in the stands behind home plate throughout the incidents — was not characterized by concern for Puerto Rico's international reputation. By far the loudest calls were to throw the protesters out of the stadium, or at least to end their protests. Creative attempts to send anti-Castro messages were persistent — a biplane with an anti-Castro banner flew by the stadium — and Ben and I met people unhappy to see political free speech suppressed inside the stadium. But they were a minority and none sat near us. The event promoters were nervous, but they had staunch allies among the vocal majority of the fans. We were surrounded by a lawyer devoted to pursuing an end to US military target practice on Vieques Island, a psychometrician and test administrator for an impor-

Figure 6. Korean fans celebrate despite semifinal defeat

tant certification exam in Puerto Rico and her husband, an advertising executive, and an Emergency Room doctor and his dental hygienist wife, who had flown back from a town on Chesapeake Bay for the WBC games. None of them wanted politics to interfere with the games; all wore some kind of Puerto Rican national hat or emblem, or waved a Puerto Rican flag whenever the occasion arose on the field. Puerto Rican nationalism was there, but funneled only through the baseball events on the field. Politics threatened to ruin what was possible there. People liked the idea that the games were being broadcast back into Cuba, that Cuban civil society was connecting to an event in Puerto Rico. But they were happy that the Cuban team was there mainly for the historic

Figure 7. San Juan police observe and protect as anti-Castro protester holds poster behind home plate

chance to beat them. When the Cubans pushed hard to remove political signs, there was no reason not to be accommodating, because, in this inverted semiosis, the games themselves meant incomparably more.

Thus in this tournament the commodity of baseball drew from world politics to heighten itself, but its main modality was the capaciousness of the game it was able to develop on the field, its power to make a new world unto itself. Unlike the Olympic movement, which has a stylized message of peace through togetherness and respect that is sufficiently impressive that the UN tried to affiliate itself to the logo of the five rings — the Olympics refused to share, see MacAloon's history — Organized Baseball does not attempt to purvey a global image or message, so far, except itself, the excellence of baseball. The

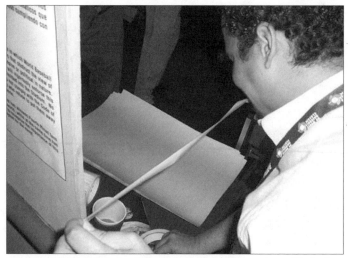

Figure 8. A WBC employee hurriedly affixes double-stick tape and posts "Code of Conduct" posters while fans enter ballpark, San Juan

only thing it offers to participating nations at the WBC is entitlement to a chance to win, and the spectacle of the attempt, against leviathans.

* * *

But why wade so deeply into the waters of nationalism? As we have seen, patriotic self-enhancement has always been part of Organized Baseball in the US. The WBC goes much farther, staging tests of national strength. Is getting this intimately involved in competing nationalisms a good idea for Organized Baseball? Not everyone in Organized Baseball thought so.

George Steinbrenner, the highly competitive, free spending Yankee owner, was particularly bitter about the tournament. Steinbrenner's team held back one or two stars explicitly (catcher Jorge Posada, at least). Some Yankees played but others refused invitations (notably outfielder Hideki Matsui, much loved by the Japanese, and great relief pitcher Mariano Rivera, missed sorely by Panama in two very close losses). Steinbrenner feared injuries and resented interference with his own team's preparations. Obviously, he opposed the WBC because he was locked in on the main chances for Yankee victory. But observing Steinbrenner's public behavior run the gamut from principled to churlish, he also seemed to speak for many other US baseball people who were disturbed by the prospect of another pinnacle tourney. Was the greater threat to the Yankees that the World Baseball Classic would injure Yankee efforts to win the World Series (by injuring or tiring key players) or was it something else — a threat to the meaning of Yankee efforts to win the World Series? Did the sensitive Steinbrenner perceive a new, fundamental threat to his chance to reach and hold the commanding heights of baseball? I think that was the larger point of his opposition all along.

"They were not prepared for the greatness of the event." Jesus Alou spoke of the US team, to William Rhoden of *The New York Times* (March 21, 2006). "Next time, they will be." There is no doubt that the US team played the tournament differently than the other teams. Especially in the first round, their attitude was closer to "spring training by other means" than pursuit of world championship. The United States was the only team to have every field player on the roster average at least one at-bat per game. Of the other seven teams who advanced, two had only ten field players average one or more plate appearance per game (Japan and Venezuela) and four of the other five had eleven players average one or more plate appearance per game. Only the Dominican Republic, which changed personnel at second base and catcher, came close to the US record, with fourteen players having one or more plate appearance per game on average. And on the Dominican roster, three other players were riding pine. Only in its last, desperate losses did the US stick with one lineup. Those who argue that Dontrelle Willis's two disastrous starts were the real story have a point, also. But I think Jesus Alou was right. How far does his assessment extend also to the Lords of the Game?

Gene Orza, Bob DuPuy and others gave many reasons for holding the tournament in Spring Training, above all, player willingness and preference. In his blog DuPuy gave a plausible explanation for why the semifinals matched teams from the same second rounds — regional championship logic, insuring appeal for regional audiences. But everything happened as if the US was determined not to meet the tough Caribbean teams, especially Cuba, until the finals. Organized Baseball did little to address the fairness of having all the US games home games, and mostly US umpires. They did not even remove US umpire Bob Davidson from the rotation after two egregious mistakes, one highly consequential, that both favored the US. Scheduling in Spring Training meant playing the Cubans toward the end of their season, and facing Caribbean players fresh from winter ball and the Caribbean Series (though in the event, apart from the Cubans few WBC players played winter ball this year, and Caribbean Series stars such as Álex González, Franklin Guttierez, and Johnny Gomes didn't make their national teams for the WBC). Many sportswriters found it curious that baseball was competing for TV time and media attention with the NCAA's basketball championships.

But if timing is everything, the single obvious point about the World Baseball Classic is that it did not come after the World Series. Ever since the days of Landis' ban on barnstorming for World Series players, the Lords of the Game have attended to the needs of their "fall classic." It needs, above all, to provide the pinnacle, the commanding heights, the

ultimate in victory — this is the very stuff of purity
and hope for the Nethercutts, and Steinbrenners, of
the world.

Thus there is an obvious politics to the
disquiet surrounding the success of the World
Baseball Classic. It was, in short, too good for
comfort. We have seen how the titling of the World
Series began with deliberate irony, coy respect for
multiple leagues each holding national championship
series. The World Baseball Classic's coyness is also
built into its title — the word "championship"
nowhere in sight.

* * *

Phoning home one night from San Diego, I
told my wife Martha Kaplan that Cuba's success posed

Figure 9. A Dominican player is interviewed, PETCO Park in San Diego

an interesting challenge to Organized Baseball, considering all the Major League stars from Venezuela, Puerto Rico, and the Dominican Republic laid waste in their wake. She pointed out that I was forgetting something, in my anthropological enthusiasm for subalterns. The real rival to US domination in baseball, from a capitalist point of view, was clearly Japan. On the field the Japanese had just about as rough a tournament as the US did, until the last few games. But there is no doubt Martha was on to something if we look at the business strategies and tactics leading into the tournament.

Cuba took some real political abuse and still entered the tournament, giving away their prize money and risking defection of their players to make it possible. Regardless what you think of Cuba's political system, note how hard they worked to be in the tournament and stay in it. The Cubans all through the games in San Juan were in a test of wills with MLB officials and with the press concerning how they should conduct themselves and be treated as performers. Proud to wield the title "amateurs" and, in a memorable bit of controversy, to be "men not names," they did not like to practice in view of the press or public, nor to be much interviewed. Their translators refused all political questions and even doctored political answers, as if there weren't other Spanish speakers in the world. WBC press officials scrambled to improve the translations to avoid further scandal.

Another politics also played out in the arrangements for interviews and for security — the question of Major League Baseball protocols versus international protocols, especially from the Olympics. The Cubans routinely cited Olympic standards when complaining about press or security issues. "This would never happen in the Olympics" was a complaint, notably, in the controversy over political placards. Baseball beat writers, meanwhile, were stunned not to have access to locker rooms. Olympics planning veterans had recommended building each team a temporary locker room compound rather than having them share locker rooms in the stadiums. But WBC officials were not ready for the expense or variation from Organized Baseball norms, so teams used stadium locker rooms, moving in and out constantly. Organized Baseball's savoir faire will be under review in the negotiations about umpires, locker rooms, press, and security accommodations for the next World Baseball Classic.

The most visible politics behind and around the World Baseball Classic involved Cuba: mollifying Cubans officials, silencing Cuba protesters, and before that just getting the visas. But a quieter disputation also merits notice, a whisper in the whirlwind. It took the leadership of Organized Baseball years to get the Japanese to agree to come to their tournament. Japanese league officials and their player's union officials had both objected to the structure and timing of the event. Organized Baseball eventually coerced them by announcing the tournament's existence, with Japan slotted in place, before negotiations were close to completion. A certain form of sabotage?

Organized Baseball and especially its Players Union talked of a professional baseball World Cup as early as Spring 2000. By then Organized Baseball had launched a modest globalization program, with two exhibition games with Cuba and early season games in Monterrey, Mexico and Tokyo, Japan. Press observers thought Organized Baseball was trying to catch up with the NBA in search of global revenue. By 2000 nativist resistance emerged, and Mark McGwire gave it voice in an interview with Murray Chass of *The New York Times* (March 21, 2000). The year before, McGwire and his Cardinal teammates refused to play the Mets in Tokyo. "I know Major League Baseball wants to do more internationally, but there is no purpose to it."

But planning went on. The Japanese vetoed a plan for a 2005 World Baseball Classic. They preferred an international hosting body, and wanted a November tournament, after the regular season. A year later the impasse continued. Nevertheless in May 2005 a joint news release from Commissioner Bud Selig and Union head Donald Fehr announced the plan for a sixteen team tournament in March 2006, including a first round group in Japan, without a list of participating nations. In June, reports surfaced that Japan might not play, following a visit to Japan by US baseball officials that failed to secure an agreement. Gene Orza adroitly explained the impasse to the US press: "I think they felt that they should have had more consultation afforded them than they believe was the case," as quoted by Barry Bloom. A somewhat more detailed account reached readers of the Yomiuri newspapers. In November 2004, representatives of Nippon Professional Baseball, the Korean

Professional League, and MLB met in Tokyo and agreed in principle to hold the World Baseball Classic including an Asian qualifying round in Tokyo. The Japanese believed the financial structure was still to be discussed, at a steering committee meeting in December. That meeting was cancelled by MLB, either "without any explanation," said Kazuo Hasegawa, secretary general of the NPB commissioner's office, or because MLB awaited a sanctioning agreement with the International Baseball Federation that came in March, said Jim Small, managing director of MLB Japan. (The IBAF, holder of the amateur baseball World Cups, through its Puerto Rican affiliate later fought to keep the Cubans in the tournament, threatening to withdraw sanction.)

When MLB announced plans in May, it said that proceeds would form a central fund later divided among participating organizations. Nippon Professional Baseball wanted instead to control the rights to promote the Asian qualifying round in Tokyo. "If we allow Japan a separate deal, it would ruin the whole business model," Jim Small explained. Indeed. Then NPB would have been a kind of partner, co-owner, and manager of some portion of the World Baseball Classic. The strategy of Organized Baseball was absolutely not to share ownership of any part of its organization with NPB. The issue then was how to get Japanese participation without real Japanese partnership. Thus the officials' visit to Japan, with the prospect of the tournament already public, and the deadline of June 30th for a Japanese participation commitment. Responding to this June

30th deadline ("the absolutely outermost limit of time we had," Orza said) the Japanese sent a counterproposal on timing and revenue on July 1st. On July 8th, something new intruded, streamlining events and building pressure on Japan.

On July 8, 2005, the International Olympic Committee voted baseball out of the Olympics, starting in 2012. Note that this decision was taken long after the upcoming, professional WBC was in planning, even in the news. Despite the obvious confluence, the Olympics abandoning a sport where they were clearly not to be the pinnacle championship, many in the baseball world were by all appearances shocked and surprised. The Cubans were the most vociferous in disappointment, blaming professional leagues and especially the US leagues for not releasing their players to the Olympic tournament. (In the 2004 Olympics, Japanese professionals played, two from each Japanese major league team. They still finished third, but defeated the Cuban gold medalists in their only head-to-head game; Matsuzaka pitched.) On July 11, 2005 the WBC organizers officially announced tournament details, with Japan among participants and games in Tokyo, despite not having a Japanese commitment in hand. On September 16th, more than two months later, the Japanese finally agreed to terms.

Of all baseball powers the Cubans and the Japanese were least happy about the business structure of the World Baseball Classic. The Cubans actually took longer to formally accept terms to play, despite their intense desire to play the US professionals, as manifest in later willingness to accommodate abusive US political moves. Both the Cubans and the Japanese were concerned that the tournament would be owned and run by Organized Baseball rather than a truly international organization. The head of the Japanese players' association, Yakult Swallows catcher Atsuya Furuta, was quoted on *ESPN.com* on September 16th, the day that the Japanese announced their agreement. "This is the first step toward playing in a truly international tournament, something our association has been longing for."

* * *

To get a final, best perspective on what is really going on, I want to finish with the sharp contrast between Atsuya Furuta and Mark McGuire's hopes for the future of baseball, and use them to consider most generally what we can conclude about game theory and games in actual capitalist practice by way of this historical study of an actual, celebrated capitalist game. Then, we will address the connected issues delineated in the second preface, about American power, beginning with Bud Selig's apparent obsession with Jackie Robinson and all those "trail-blazer" videos. I will give the last word to Cuban manager Higinio Velez. But now I want to bring back Mark McGwire to explain why, in his view, international play is worse than unnecessary.

Mark McGwire's more recent steroids testimony has rendered him one of baseball's less deep thinkers as well as one of its great players and show-men. But McGwire had a clear sense of baseball's present and future, in his March 21, 2000 interview with Murray Chass. He said:

> I take the game seriously. To me, to go play world-wide doesn't turn my crank. I want to play here in America. I have nothing against anybody else in another country. This game belongs here. People come to America, they come here to watch our game.

When Japan and Cuba won the WBC semifinals, much was made of the absence of Major Leaguers from the final. Only two players on the finals rosters, both playing for Japan, were US Major Leaguers. McGwire is hardly alone, however, in his ability to overlook the long history of excellent baseball elsewhere. Throughout the WBC scoreboards displayed the quotation from Bud Selig that opens this section, implying that the world just recently began to compete in America's game. The display implied that the WBC was recognition that Organized Baseball did not own the game, when in practice it was precisely a takeover. The day after Japan's victory, journalists like Jim Caple of *ESPN.com* could begin articles every bit as sanguine as McGwire about Major League centrality in the baseball world. Caple wrote, "Cheer up, fellow Americans. Our country might not have even reached the final round of the World Baseball Classic, but the best players eventually all wind up here." (Caple wrote, in particular, about the expected MLB arrival of Daisuke Matsuzaka.)

International sport has its own dialogics. Planners for professional basketball and baseball can see the soccer/football world stretched between its leagues, champions' league and World Cup nationalism. It can see that European teams gather the world's talent, but not all the profits because they don't own the soccer World Cup. Officials of Organized Baseball can see global basketball revenues sparked by the NBA's "dream team" Olympic appearance, but also the catastrophe of the "nightmare team" that followed. Stagnation for NBA globalism follows, again, from not owning the world championship. So Organized Baseball built the World Baseball Classic. It persuaded everyone to come. Were they prepared, after all, for the greatness of the event?

The reason why Organized Baseball's management could not simply take McGwire's advice and stay home, was in part as McGwire suggested, that there was a great deal of money to be made. Not least is the merchandizing, at the synergy of baseball and nationalism. The other dimension of opportunity and risk was that the game was internationalizing within Organized Baseball. More than 29.2% of MLB rosters and 45.4% of minor league rosters in 2005 were players from outside the US. McGwire was right that people come to the US for baseball. But this actually constituted a new pinnacle problem, and particular stresses that the World Baseball Classic is, precisely, all about. Breton and Villegas poignantly document in their book, *Away Games*, that for young Caribbean players in the US, all the games are away games. As noted earlier, the flow of Japanese players is particularly interesting because pay cuts are often involved. Most Japanese stars have not left Japan.

Increasing numbers of Caribbean players head to East Asia to play their life of "away games." And as the comment by Furuta, head of the Japanese Player's Association should remind us, the Japanese are perfectly capable of taking the initiative in capitalist business ventures also. The World Baseball Classic may have proved W. P. Kinsella's *Field of Dreams* adage, "build it and they will come." But if Organized Baseball hadn't built it, soon, in all likelihood someone else would have tried. In fact, Organized Baseball is actually presented with multiple opportunities to internationalize far more than it has, more than it is willing to. Instead, it acts creatively to sustain a particular, highly American, style of international interaction, as much to its own benefit as possible.

Here, then, we can draw our final conclusions about games in general as we contrast the very particular visions of the future of this game from McGwire and Furuta. McGwire likes it like he has it (or had it), and probably speaks for a wide and deep vein of US baseball sentiment — from Steinbrenner to many a barroom philosopher, or to Karl Ravech — when McGwire declares that baseball "belongs here." He has nothing against foreigners, but he takes the game seriously, as Ravech also did, no doubt, when he depicted the WBC as a chance for the US to "reclaim the game" (on the ESPN *Sportscenter* broadcast on March 7, 2006, as the US began play in the WBC). At another level, as I have argued, this was surely the goal of Organized Baseball's leadership also: to reclaim ownership of the game precisely by risking mastery on the field. As Ruth Benedict reported long ago, "lose to win" is a popular Japanese aphorism. But it better represents the strategy of Organized Baseball in the WBC. The US lost on the field, but Organized Baseball recaptured absolute ownership of the pinnacle of baseball competition.

Atsuya Furuta framed the WBC as something else, merely a "first step" toward an actually international future that his association "has been longing for." In the first preface I argued that the modern prince is real games: this was of course a rephrasing of Gramsci's conviction that political parties were "the modern prince," capable of changing the world. The great power of game theory to inform strategies and define positions is never absolute, and its reductions are precisely their weakest where the whirlwinds are the most whisper-filled, which often happens when other games are also being played. Thus corporate capitalism is not only about capacious reason, as Weber saw most coherently, but also, as Veblen saw most acutely, about controlling the framing and staging of commodity transactions, about controlling the terms of trade, the rules of the game. Making the world safe for your game. Thus, far from being about commodities and their production, circulation, and consumption, real capitalism especially in Veblen's New Order is all about controlling and influencing the future of real commodiousness, vested interests being precisely the commanding heights of definition of the world's best things and their rules for disposition. Learning to analyze as a game the creation and manipulation of such rules is very helpful, but not failsafe in a world where others, also, are both analysts and players. Empires, even political parties, are not the most advanced tools in the politics of this economics, nation-state boundaries placing far more limits on the reach of political parties than corporations, while limited liability has made the world safe for playing serious games.

Selig, Orza, Dupuy, and the rest of the leadership of Organized Baseball took measurable risks in the WBC, aware of the resistance of McGwire, Steinbrenner et al, and of the size of the budget devoted to the project; they also faced risks harder to reckon, for example the goodwill of politicians, fans, and some players. Perhaps the risk most difficult to address, in the end, will be what Alou called "the greatness of the event." They were certainly prepared for it, in the sense that they chose Spring Training and limited the pitching, named it "classic," not championship, and so on. But just as, following Weber, friction and opacity set limits on the state's power to regulate the changes to the world rendered by large scale corporations, so also the reality of their games set limits to the power of even the best organized of corporations (a title few would give Organized Baseball; see just about any labor history). As anthropologists are no doubt better positioned than economists to appreciate, more happens when you change the world than any modeling can anticipate, and as Furuta's comments made visible, more games than one, seeing different steps toward different goals, can be real simultaneously.

How, then, does the nascent success of the WBC connect to what Martha Kaplan and I have called "the end of the beginning" of the era of nation-states? How does the effort of Organized Baseball to make the world safe for their brand of their game fit into the much disrupted reality of the nation-state world, sixty years into its effort to make separate-but-equal work as the organizing principle of world politics?

* * *

Bud Selig is now, internationally, the spokesperson for what I will call the Jackie Robinsonization of international baseball. The stories highlighted, over and over during the World Baseball Classic, were the "trailblazer" elegies of the lone individual, crossing boundaries and lines to enter into the leagues and games of Organized Baseball. The trailblazer tested his strength (always a he, so far) as the lonely risktaker, cutting a path for more guys to follow. Sort of like the old west, meaning cowboys, not Europe, foreign cowboys blazing new trails on the baseball range. In this fantasy they colonize Mark McGwire's team, not vice versa. There was no Cuban trailblazer video, possibly to avoid controversy over official representation of "defection." This absence was ironically appropriate anyway, given the long history of the Cuban game and longstanding presence of Cubans in Organized Baseball. It was also incongruous, since stories like El Duque's long transit by sea merited the "trailblazer" label better than most. Another absence was more subtle, but to me more profound. No stories were told about great past games or teams anywhere else in the world, none whatsoever.

In the 1940s Organized Baseball kept the Mexican League from becoming another Major League. To an observer like Jesus Alou there was always something unreal about the World Series. "All through my career — and I played in two World Series — I kept telling myself, This is not the World Series," Alou told Rhoden. In 1952, the Pacific Coast League joined the structure of Organized Baseball originally as a league of "open" classification, neither major nor minor. Not until the Dodgers and Giants moved west did its move to minor league status become inevitable. But the original fork, the dilemma to be major or minor, came from the pressure of the existence and utility of the Organized Baseball structure.

Will Organized Baseball actually expand to conquer the world? Is it already some kind of empire of baseball nations? Will it somehow turn leagues everywhere into minor leagues, give them all tidy designations, even make their franchises into farm clubs of Major League teams? It never happened in the Caribbean leagues. Something very different happened, something much more like "separate but equal" as actually practiced in the Jim Crow south, that is to say, actually profoundly unequal. But in the UN world it is a matter of nations, not races. As the nation-state system was routinized after World War II, Organized Baseball moved to fill a newly integrated space of the nation, via racial integration and as its major league franchises moved south and west. But in the Mexican League crisis, led by Happy Chandler, it profoundly rejected recognition as Major

League of any baseball anywhere else — or, any other exactly calibrated leagues, for that matter. This is not conquest, or empire; it is something else, exclusion, separation, not empire in denial but more radical denial of opportunity. Keeping things separate kept them more commodious, more comfortable and meaningful, as if it kept them pure. Each nation-state, in baseball's new world order pioneered in the Caribbean leagues, got its own pinnacle league. Teams from those leagues can enter regional championship competitions, perhaps, as was begun in the Caribbean in 1949, at least for the leagues that cooperated. Since 1994 the Asian Games have provided a regional tournament for Asian teams. But teams from elsewhere do not get real championship games with the Yankees, Cardinals, Red Sox, or White Sox. Not on the agenda. Equal may never be known, for the Tokyo Giants, Yakult Swallows, or Chiba Lotte Marines, because separate is for sure. Yes, it was terrible when color lines denied basic opportunities on the basis of race. Pedro Lazo is now thirty-three years old.

The pressures that build when substantive differences and inequalities are visible across the porous but well-staked international boundaries, are the pressures that lead to diaspora. Organized Baseball would like the solution to be migration, the stories to all be Jackie Robinsonades.

The trailblazer videos generated cheers for local heroes in San Juan. But the crowds responded variously to individuals depicted and not noticeably to the overall message. The trailblazer story mixes metaphors poorly with the industrial, plantation orga-

nization of the actual baseball academies that
Organized Baseball has built, especially in Venezuela
and the Dominican Republic. These actual farms for
the growing of talent are more autarkic even than
Rickey's vertical system. The "academies" bring players inside the fences, and observe them, for years.
They are rigorously separate, private, not an integrated piece of local baseball.

The actual "trailblazers" carve trails through
security gates in walls and wire, like the wire at the
camps designed to keep people out. The game space
is enhanced and protected by control of many kinds
at many levels. Pace Agamben, the sign of our times
of Pax Americana is not the bare life of the refugee
camp. The states whose walls kept populations in
have mostly collapsed in the late twentieth century,
starting with the Berlin Wall. But we are in the era of
endless ramification of security systems that keep
people out, defending zones of privilege. At airports,
the US elite even screens itself obsessively, endlessly
requiring rituals of recognition, redefining freedom as
entitlement to enter secure oases and other kinds of
purer and more commodious space. Some of the
Dodger players, in 1947, wanted to sustain the purity
of absolute color lines, separate but equal race exclusion, especially the separate part (the "but equal" was
the court's effort to place such things accord with
"equal protection under the law"). Durocher says he
told them why they couldn't:

> They're good athletes and there's nowhere else
> they can make this kind of money. They're going

> to come, boys, and they're going to come scratch-
> ing and diving. Unless you fellows lookout and
> wake up, they're going to run you right out of the
> ball park.

Organized Baseball has succeeded, so far, in requiring these players to come to the US as lonely individuals, fantasy loners controlled by contractual arrangements and mutual recognitions. Organized Baseball now recognizes Japanese baseball's reserve system, which allows players under Japanese contract to leave organizations as free agents, for example to sign with US teams, only after nine years. Thus everyone knows that Daisuke Matsuzaka looks forward to 2008 (Robert Whiting notes his plans in his 2004 book *The Meaning of Ichiro*).

Organized Baseball has the means to sponsor another excellent World Baseball Classic in 2009. To do so, it will have to convince the Japanese not to design an even better one, in November rather than March. During ESPN's broadcast of the WBC final, Peter Gammons argued that the WBC could only be held in the US, because the US is now so cosmopolitan and multicultural. Looking closely, we can see how this too, this diasporic America, is a consequence of the pressures of American plans realized in the UN era, this new world order. More than baseball has been Jackie Robinsonized. Individuals and families migrate, world structural inequalities addressed by people voting with their feet. But here race and nation have fundamentally different stories to tell. The Jackie Robinson story was supposed to mean the end of barriers and integration, as Robinson himself argued in his book *Baseball Has Done It*. Though racism hasn't been ended in fact, many color lines were certainly erased in law. Diasporic migration does not end the difference of nation-states, and nation-states are still the primary vehicles of civil rights in law. Their boundaries are more fiercely patrolled than ever — or at least, those of the US are.

By owning the WBC Organized Baseball sustains its own ability to manage its global position. It can generate massive new revenues in the long run, and it has more hope of keeping other baseball powers from organizing something different: like another Major League. If Organized Baseball can continue on this path, the WBC will be a lucrative spectacle, a vast, high-level tryout camp, and a safety valve for global baseball aspirations. It allows Organized Baseball's formidable Others to get very close, perhaps just close enough, to an actual chance to beat the Yankees at their own game.

Branch Rickey considered trying the talented Cuban Silvio Garcia as the first black Major Leaguer, but he already had a shortstop, and he feared that a foreigner couldn't garner the sympathy necessary for the lonely man strategy to work. Another choice was obvious, but apparently Rickey never approached him: Satchel Paige. One reason why Paige was not asked was that Paige had already declared that he would not consider entering Organized Baseball by himself. Paige was entirely willing to play in the Major Leagues. Eventually, when other blacks were established there, he entered as an individual. But as a younger man, before Jackie Robinson's glory years, Paige was clear and outspoken on what it would take to get him into the Majors: his whole team. If the Major Leagues would let in the Kansas City Monarchs, Paige was ready.

The World Baseball Classic is a "break-though," to borrow another of Jesus Alou's words. It creates a new pinnacle for baseball play, regardless of efforts to keep it spring training by other means. How serious and how central the tournament becomes is not something Organized Baseball can entirely control. An actual threat to the status of the World Series is understood by many. But at the same time, the WBC allows Organized Baseball to sustain the structures that constitute its inner purity, maintaining the boundaries of its regular and post seasons above all against all challenge by foreign teams, all the while increasing its global reach in recruiting talent and vending its commodity. The Tokyo Giants and the Chiba Lotte Marines, the Havana Industriales and the Santiago Avispas, the Caracas Lions and the Licey Tigers, all the champions and perennial powers of the world's other leading leagues, need not apply. That is the state of the baseball world today, and the shape of the vested interest that controls and limits its development. To call it an empire, or even a monopoly, is to seriously underestimate it. It is to fail to see the form of power it wields in shaping the separateness of its own commodious world, controlling access, avoiding and deflecting competition, limiting liability, sustaining and elaborating fictions of separate but equal, and mostly separate.

When the press at the WBC did get the chance to speak with the Cubans, the one thing they wanted to discuss above all was politics, but baseball politics. There is only one real issue in Cuba-US baseball politics, if you listen to most of the US writers. True, writers asked other political questions, about players' views on Castro and socialism. But those things were interesting really only as means to the more fundamental baseball political question: the availability of Cuban players for the teams in Organized Baseball. The strength of the players is obvious, the successes of other Cuban players well known. Cuban manager Higinio Velez turned the topic, in many World Baseball Classic interviews, toward pleas for more international venues for Cuban teams to play. Velez and Organized Baseball volleyed on these subjects publicly as well as privately. Velez argued on many occasions for more frequent WBC. Gene Orza told the press that bi-annual World Baseball Classics were financially and logistically impossible. Velez wants Olympic baseball back with professionals included as well. Asked if Cuba would send a champion to the Caribbean Series, he said, in the WBC formal interview of March 12th, "We're always ready, we're just awaiting an invitation. We have the desire, the wishes, and just let us know. We're always willing to do it." The dominant position already achieved by the World Baseball Classic in Caribbean baseball, a beginning of hegemony, was clear in one of Velez's more poignant comments. Velez explained to ESPN's Enrique Rojas that Cuba could host a round in the next WBC (an idea Orza

thought possible, as long as it was a first round pool).
"Hosting games in the next event is the maximum
ambition that any country that loves baseball could
have," Velez said.

Participation in the WBC, hosting a round, as
the maximum ambition for a ballplaying nation. This
is half, I argue, of Organized Baseball's dream, articulated in the extreme, from an extreme. But with the
other half, and perhaps the larger half, the issue of
access to the players, another story emerged. Velez
predicted correctly that no Cuban players would
defect, especially because the team would be greeted
as heroes on return, and also because none wanted to
anyway. The tightness of Cuban security belied the
confidence of Cuban rhetoric. But he also said something else, something that, for me, flashed up the
memory of Satchel Paige and his beloved and formidable Monarchs, in the present political moment. For
all of our ease in understanding objections to racism,
for all that we can see the flaws in separate but equal
when it generated the Major Leagues and the Negro
Leagues, most of us now, not only but especially
Americans, have no inkling how strange and immoral
will someday seem our sanguine acceptance of the
legal fortresses of limited liability and nation-state
self-determination. Velez was asked, in his final
formal WBC interview after the loss to Japan, "Do
you feel that there are players on your team that
could play in the major leagues, and would you hope
one day that the relations might change and allow
Cuban players to play in the major leagues?" And he
said, "Cuba, regarding the fact that it could be part of

the major leagues, that's not for me to say. It is up to you." ▦

Figure 10. Pedro Lazo pitches to Miguel Tejada, WBC semifinal.

Acknowledgements

Many people have helped me with this project. Benjamin Eastman accompanied me to the World Baseball Classic games in San Juan and San Diego, pursuing his own research and also helping with mine; our ongoing conversations have greatly improved my understanding of Cuban and Latin American baseball, and of international sports, and his acute observations on this essay in manuscript have greatly improved this text. Ben and I both thank the support staff of the Baseball World Classic for allowing us access and interviews and providing us with invaluable information about the players and games. Fans in and around the stands in both San Juan and San Diego were extraordinarily gracious, even when the arcane rules of human subjects research required us to launch into full explanations of our presence, purposes, and methods while we were all trying to watch and appreciate some really excellent baseball games. Baseball journalists, who in their refreshingly piratical style absolutely lacked the fans' patience and almost invariably cut off our briefest explanations of our research goals and methods, were also wonderful interlocutors in fact.

Thanks to the staff of the National Baseball Hall of Fame in Cooperstown for their aid in my research there after the WBC, and to my daughter Nory for her aid in that research. Thanks to Emiko Ohnuki-Tierney for her collegial assistance in locating and translating information about Eiji Sawamura and Japanese baseball history, and to Robert Fitts for help in locating the photograph of Eiji Sawamura. And thanks to Marshall Sahlins and the Prickly Paradigm Press for inspiring the project and to Matthew Engelke for excellent editing.

Thanks to Nory also for taping WBC games for me, and to my daughter Rosie for watching many a game with me. Martha as usual read everything and helped shape this project from the first proposal to this last word.

Also available from Prickly Paradigm Press:

continued